RWANDA: DEMOCRACY THWARTED

HEARING

BEFORE THE

SUBCOMMITTEE ON AFRICA, GLOBAL HEALTH, GLOBAL HUMAN RIGHTS, AND INTERNATIONAL ORGANIZATIONS

OF THE

COMMITTEE ON FOREIGN AFFAIRS
HOUSE OF REPRESENTATIVES

ONE HUNDRED FIFTEENTH CONGRESS

FIRST SESSION

SEPTEMBER 27, 2017

I0776346

Serial No. 115–70

Printed for the use of the Committee on Foreign Affairs

Available via the World Wide Web: http://www.foreignaffairs.house.gov/ or http://www.gpo.gov/fdsys/

U.S. GOVERNMENT PUBLISHING OFFICE

27–012PDF   WASHINGTON : 2017

COMMITTEE ON FOREIGN AFFAIRS

EDWARD R. ROYCE, California, *Chairman*

CHRISTOPHER H. SMITH, New Jersey
ILEANA ROS-LEHTINEN, Florida
DANA ROHRABACHER, California
STEVE CHABOT, Ohio
JOE WILSON, South Carolina
MICHAEL T. McCAUL, Texas
TED POE, Texas
DARRELL E. ISSA, California
TOM MARINO, Pennsylvania
JEFF DUNCAN, South Carolina
MO BROOKS, Alabama
PAUL COOK, California
SCOTT PERRY, Pennsylvania
RON DeSANTIS, Florida
MARK MEADOWS, North Carolina
TED S. YOHO, Florida
ADAM KINZINGER, Illinois
LEE M. ZELDIN, New York
DANIEL M. DONOVAN, Jr., New York
F. JAMES SENSENBRENNER, Jr.,
 Wisconsin
ANN WAGNER, Missouri
BRIAN J. MAST, Florida
FRANCIS ROONEY, Florida
BRIAN K. FITZPATRICK, Pennsylvania
THOMAS A. GARRETT, Jr., Virginia

ELIOT L. ENGEL, New York
BRAD SHERMAN, California
GREGORY W. MEEKS, New York
ALBIO SIRES, New Jersey
GERALD E. CONNOLLY, Virginia
THEODORE E. DEUTCH, Florida
KAREN BASS, California
WILLIAM R. KEATING, Massachusetts
DAVID N. CICILLINE, Rhode Island
AMI BERA, California
LOIS FRANKEL, Florida
TULSI GABBARD, Hawaii
JOAQUIN CASTRO, Texas
ROBIN L. KELLY, Illinois
BRENDAN F. BOYLE, Pennsylvania
DINA TITUS, Nevada
NORMA J. TORRES, California
BRADLEY SCOTT SCHNEIDER, Illinois
THOMAS R. SUOZZI, New York
ADRIANO ESPAILLAT, New York
TED LIEU, California

Amy Porter, *Chief of Staff*   Thomas Sheehy, *Staff Director*
Jason Steinbaum, *Democratic Staff Director*

Subcommittee on Africa, Global Health, Global Human Rights, and International Organizations

CHRISTOPHER H. SMITH, New Jersey, *Chairman*

MARK MEADOWS, North Carolina
DANIEL M. DONOVAN, Jr., New York
F. JAMES SENSENBRENNER, Jr.,
 Wisconsin
THOMAS A. GARRETT, Jr., Virginia

KAREN BASS, California
AMI BERA, California
JOAQUIN CASTRO, Texas
THOMAS R. SUOZZI, New York

CONTENTS

Page

WITNESSES

LETTERS, STATEMENTS, ETC., SUBMITTED FOR THE HEARING

APPENDIX

RWANDA: DEMOCRACY THWARTED

HOUSE OF REPRESENTATIVES,
SUBCOMMITTEE ON AFRICA, GLOBAL HEALTH,
GLOBAL HUMAN RIGHTS, AND INTERNATIONAL ORGANIZATIONS,
COMMITTEE ON FOREIGN AFFAIRS,
Washington, DC.

The subcommittee met, pursuant to notice, at 3:00 p.m., in room 2200 Rayburn House Office Building, Hon. Christopher H. Smith (chairman of the subcommittee) presiding.

Mr. SMITH. The subcommittee will come to order, and good afternoon to everybody.

Rwanda is an important African ally. We know it. They have been for a very long time. This East African nation has been a valuable contributor to peacekeeping in Africa and is the sixth largest troop and police contributor to U.N. missions.

However, reports have increased about the status of human rights and rule of law inside Rwanda and its efforts to silence critics living abroad.

This hearing will continue to examine the future of democracy and the rule of law in Rwanda in light of persistent criticism of its government's behavior at home and on the international stage.

Rwanda is a constitutional republic dominated by a very strong presidency. In 2015, the country held a constitutional referendum in which an estimated 98 percent of registered voters participated.

Approximately 98 percent of those who voted endorsed a set of amendments that included provisions that would allow the President to run for up to three additional terms in office, meaning Paul Kagame could be President for more than 20 more years.

His election to a third term in August 2017 was achieved with 99 percent of the vote. A popular politician in the United States and most other countries would be unlikely in most circumstances to win nearly 100 percent of the vote in a free, fair, and competitive election.

Consequently, it is difficult to believe that even someone as widely admired as President Kagame could have been that popular.

Such suspicion is stoked by reports of vote irregularities and actions by the Rwandan Government to restrain opposition activism and enact stringent controls on opposition activism including legal restrictions on civil liberties and stringent controls on the free flow of information.

An example of why there is skepticism about the nature of free elections in Rwanda is the case of businesswoman Diane Rwigara, who ran as a critic of Kagame.

Days after she launched her campaign, nude photos allegedly of her were leaked onto the internet in an attempt to discredit her. She said she would not be intimidated and continued her campaign.

On July 7th, the National Electoral Commission disqualified her and two other candidates on technical grounds, alleging they had not collected enough valid signatures.

Amnesty International said that the election would be held in a climate of fear and repression, and the Commission's decision was criticized by the U.S. State Department as well as the European Union.

Following the election, Rwigara launched an activist group called the People's Salvation movement to challenge the regime on its human rights record, saying that the country's Parliament is little more than a rubber stamp.

Within days, her home was raided and she was arrested for forgery and tax evasion. Within days, although she was released, Rwigara was rearrested for forgery and offenses against state security. Her mothers and her sisters were also subsequently arrested for tax evasion.

This is not the only case of harsh punishment of those who criticise the Kagame government. David Himbara, one of our witnesses today, was a close advisor to President Kagame and has an inside view of how this government deals with those seen as failing the government or those who disagree with it.

He testified on the inner workings of the Kagame government at our May 20, 2015 hearing on Rwanda. Another witness at that May 2015 hearing was Robert Higiro, who told a chilling account of being solicited to commit murders of two formerly high-ranking military and security officials.

That account was backed by authenticated recordings of Rwanda's security chief offering large sums of money for the murders. In fact, after Mr. Higiro testified about his offer, he had to move from Belgium to the United States because his life was in danger.

Both of our Rwandan witnesses have new information today that will be important for our Government's policy toward Rwanda.

During a staff delegation to South Africa last year, two of my staff spoke with officials of the Government of South Africa, which was highly offended that the Rwandan Government would be involved in the murder of a dissident on New Year's Eve 2013.

My staff also spoke with Rwandan refugees in South Africa who reported being afraid of officials at the Rwandan Embassy in South Africa who said they had threatened them for seeking asylum.

Again, Rwanda is not your typical dictatorship in which all people suffer under an unpopular leader who does not provide for social services or security.

Many Rwandans apparently generally feel the government is acting in their interests, especially providing for interethnic harmony.

It is this anomaly that we seek to better understand in part through this hearing today. My office has compiled a report on our

Government's human rights issues with Rwanda and we are due to discuss these matters with them further.

We would be a poor ally if we did not caution the Rwandan Government about human rights abuses which the international community cites.

And so I would just conclude, in reading over all the testimony I just thought there were a number of important points made by all of our witnesses. But Amnesty International, I think, really brought home the fact that numerous journalists have been imprisoned. The Rwandan Government continues to suppress the independence and freedom of the media. This is from their testimony for today.

They also point out that the international community including the Clinton, the Bush, and the Obama administrations have been at best half-hearted in confronting President Kagame and pressing the Rwandan Government to reform its policy regarding human rights and political space.

I would like to now yield to my friend and colleague, Karen Bass.

Ms. BASS. Thank you, Mr. Chair.

As always, thank you for your leadership in holding today's hearing on developments in Rwanda, especially regarding examining democratic practices.

While Rwanda is geographically a small nation, its condition and role in the stability of the Great Lakes region is critical.

I also want to thank our distinguished witnesses today including the Honorable Donald Yamamoto. We are happy you're here representing the State Department. I do hope you won't be acting forever.

Several members of the Rwanda diaspora and the international human rights community—I look forward to hearing your various perspectives on both the successes and challenges of democracy in Rwanda.

Chairman Smith, I believe, very clearly laid out many of the challenges and while I know that there are many challenges across Africa and while it is very important to address the challenges and concerns it is also important to talk about where there have been some positive developments, especially given Rwanda's history.

Rwanda experienced a very dark time in '94 when over 800,000 people lost their lives. The aftermath of the '94 genocide left the physical infrastructure and political institutions destroyed.

The country lost skilled human resources and was left with a dilapidated economy. Since that time, Rwanda has exhibited a rare degree of internal stability and economic growth in a sub region marked by armed conflict and violent transfers of power.

Over the last 23 years, Rwanda has sought to change the course of the nation and embarked on an active effort to improve citizens' health, boost agricultural output, promote investment, and increase women's participation.

I do have to note that Rwanda is a world leader in women's representation with over 64 percent of Parliament being women, and that is compared to the United States, which is 18 percent.

Additionally, Rwanda has experienced an average of 7.6 percent growth per year over the last decade and this is in part due to the pro investor policies, and Rwanda scores very well on the World

Bank's Doing Business Report, ranking 56 out of 190 economies assessed in 2017 and number two in sub-Saharan Africa.

According to the WHO, the World Health Organization, between 1990 and 2016 life expectancy increased from 48 to 66 years. The mortality rate of children fell from 152 to 42 deaths per 1,000 live births and the maternal mortality rate decreased from 1,300 deaths to 290 per 100,000. Literacy levels in the country for both men and women are at nearly 70 percent.

Rwanda also plays a major role in peacekeeping across Africa and Rwandan troops participate in multiple U.N. and African Union missions.

Rwanda's peacekeepers are reportedly particularly valued because of their training and discipline. So the country has come a long way.

In spite of the progress, though, there has been a great deal of concern over Rwanda's history of unilateral intervention in the sub region and about restrictive political environment.

Rwanda has the potential to be a strong regional leader but to do this, like all countries, it must continue to address its internal challenges.

For the country's own success, it should create a space for freedom of expression, ensure the free flow of information in the country and seek A.U. or U.N. authorization or mediation when dealing with neighboring countries.

I yield back my time, Mr. Chair.

Mr. SMITH. I would like to now welcome back to the subcommittee the very distinguished Donald Y. Yamamoto, who is serving as the acting Assistant Secretary of State in the Bureau of African Affairs at the U.S. Department of State.

He has served as the Principal Deputy Assistant Secretary of State in the Bureau of African Affairs from 2003 to 2006. He was responsible for coordinating U.S. policy toward more than 20 countries in East and Central Africa.

He served as U.S. Ambassador to Ethiopia from 2006 to 2009 and U.S. Ambassador to the Republic of Djibouti from 2000 to 2003, and he has testified many, many times before this committee and he is more than welcome.

Mr. Ambassador, please proceed as you would like.

STATEMENT OF THE HONORABLE DONALD YAMAMOTO, ACTING ASSISTANT SECRETARY, BUREAU OF AFRICAN AFFAIRS, U.S. DEPARTMENT OF STATE

Mr. YAMAMOTO. Thank you very much. I submit the longer form for the record.

Mr. SMITH. Sure. Without objection, so ordered.

Mr. YAMAMOTO. Mr. Chairman and Ranking Member Bass, thank you for the invitation today.

Since the United States has a very close and complex relationship with Rwanda, since rebuilding the country in 1994 genocide, over the last 23 years Rwanda has made remarkable gains in recovering from this tragedy.

At the same time, Rwanda's record in the areas of human rights and democracy, while improved in some areas, remains a concern.

U.S. policy toward Rwanda seeks to support those areas where the government continues to make progress and urges the government to effect change where it needs to do more, especially in the expanding space of political dialogue and competition to take steps toward democratic transition of power.

Since the genocide, Rwanda's progress in the fields of health and development have been dramatic and we have been proud to partner in this process.

Over the last decade, child mortality has been reduced by two-thirds. Life expectancy has risen to 64½ years of age by 2016.

HIV prevalence has dropped from a little under 5 percent to 3 percent in the same period, and with support for the President's Emergency Plan for AIDS and Relief, PEPFAR, the Government of Rwanda has reduced HIV transmission to newborns to just 2 percent.

Likewise, the economic growth and opportunity have been important aspects of our partnership with Rwanda over the past—over the past 20 years.

In the last two decades, Rwanda's economic growth has averaged about 7 to 8 percent, making it one of the leading countries, according to the World Bank.

Rwanda is a major contributor to regional peace and security. It is now the fifth largest contributor to peacekeeping operations, and of course third in police operations. Rwandan troops are regionally respected and disciplined and participate in peacekeeping operations.

In South Sudan, Rwanda recently deployed additional peacekeeping troops as part of the U.N.'s Regional Protection Force and Rwanda is a priority partner in reforming the African Union so that it is better prepared to resolve regional conflicts. And President Kagame will take over the rotating chairmanship of the African Union in January 2018.

Despite these positive areas, we continue to have concerns—serious concerns about weak democratic institutions, freedom of speech, respect for human rights in Rwanda.

There have been several important developments since the subcommittee's last similarly-themed hearing on Rwanda in May 2015. In December 2015, Rwanda's voters approved a package of constitutional amendments including one that enabled President Kagame to stay in power beyond the two-term limit contained in Rwanda's constitution.

In the run-up of that decision, we engaged in extensive public and private diplomacy, urging the President to honor the commitment he made in respect to term limits when he first assumed office.

The constitutional amendments allowed President Kagame, who had been in office since 2000, to run for a third term.

We continue to publically and privately emphasize our conviction that constitutional transition of power are essential for strong democracies everywhere and the efforts by incumbents to change rules to stay in power will weaken democratic institutions and undermine long-term stability.

The August 4th Presidential elections illustrate that democracy in Rwanda remains far from perfect. As you know, the President was reelected in an official tally of nearly 99 percent of the vote.

In the August 5th statement, we said we were disturbed by the voting irregularities we had observed and reiterated our longstanding concerns over the integrity of the vote-counting process.

Three aspiring candidates were disqualified before the election and we expressed concern of the lack of transparency in the process.

We noted in our statement we hoped that these concerns will be addressed before the 2018 parliamentary elections. Compared to the previous Presidential elections in 2010, however, we noted some progress.

This was the first election in which the Democratic Green Party, the main registered opposition party in Rwanda, was allowed to participate.

The Rwandan media has reported on the harassment of some opposition candidates and government officials took action to address complaints some cases by arresting local officials.

Since the election, Rwandan officials have targeted several political opposition figures for questioning or arrest, and we are concerned by, and are following closely, the case of Diane Rwigara, one of the three disqualified Presidential aspirants. Police raided her home on August 29th, arrested Ms. Rwigara and two of her family members on September 23. We understand that the Rwandan authorities have until September 28th to press charges. In addition, we are following the arrests of at least 10 officials and members of an unregistered opposition party earlier this month. The cases suggest that tight restrictions remain on political competition and critics of the ruling party.

Other serious human rights violations have been cited in our reports to Congress and include arbitrary and unlawful killings, the security forces' disregard for the rule of law, restrictions on civil society organizations, government interference with the press. Over the years, Rwandans have reported to us the disappearance and suspected death of family members at the hands of the Rwandan security services. NGOs critical of the government are routinely denied registration to operate in the country. Government officials have also questioned, threatened, and arrested journalists who express critical views on sensitive topics. The government has used law criminalizing genocide ideology and divisionism along with national security provisions to suppress dissent, prosecute journalists, and pressure human rights groups to refrain from investigating and reporting on the findings.

The administration continues to take action to address these human rights situations in Rwanda. In March 2017, our Ambassador in Kigali initiated quarterly high-level dialogues with the government on civil society and media freedom.

USAID supports a number of targeted activities to promote the rule of law. Some areas where we continue to work include strengthening local NGO capacity to engage in policymaking improvements and to laws governing NGOs, increasing the capacity and skills of the media to provide independent impartial information, and skills training for judges.

Rwanda benefits from the African Growth and Opportunity Act (AGOA) and we have raised concerns to the Rwandan Government regarding harassment of political opposition leaders and NGOs as well as restrictions on media freedom with the context of AGOA eligibility.

We are responding to Rwanda's request for help to combat trafficking in persons, including improving prosecution skills and closing gaps, and over the last decade we have worked closely with the Rwandan Government, civil society, private sector to combat child labor and thanks to our partnership, approximately 5,000 children were removed from child labor in Rwanda's tea-growing districts between 2015 and 2017 alone.

I would like to note some good news with respect to human rights and governance in Rwanda. The Government of Rwanda holds public officials accountable for corrupt practices including through prosecution.

Rwanda has also prioritized the fight against gender-based violence and generally respects the rights of LGBTI persons.

Women leaders are promoted as evidenced by the fact, as the Congresswoman stated, that 63 percent of Parliament members and 40 percent of cabinet officials are female.

Human rights are part and parcel of our ongoing dialogue at all levels of the Rwandan Government and our consistent message remains that allowing opposition figures, journalists, and civil society to contribute to Rwanda's future is crucial to building a knowledge-based economy and government seeks to foster.

This includes ensuring freedom of expression, press freedom, ability of citizens to criticize the government and ruling party without fear of threats or violence or intimidation.

And with that, I defer to you, Mr. Congressman.

[The prepared statement of Mr. Yamamoto follows:]

Statement by Acting Assistant Secretary Donald Yamamoto,
Bureau of African Affairs
"Rwanda: Democracy Thwarted"
House Foreign Affairs Committee
Subcommittee on Africa, Global Health, Global Human Rights,
and International Organizations

Wednesday, September 27, 2017, 3:00PM

Mr. Chairman, Ranking Member Bass, and Members of the Committee,

Thank you for the invitation to testify today on U.S. efforts to support democracy in Rwanda. Democracy, along with good governance, is one of the four strategic purposes that guide our engagement with our African partners, together with increasing economic growth and investment, advancing peace and security, and countering the scourge of terrorism.

The United States has a close but complex relationship with Rwanda. The country has striven to rebuild after the 1994 genocide in which more than 800,000 people were killed in the span of about 100 days. Over the past 23 years, Rwanda has made remarkable gains in recovering from this tragedy.

At the same time, Rwanda's record in the areas of human rights and democracy, while improved in some areas, remains a concern. U.S. policy toward Rwanda seeks to support those areas where the government continues to make progress, and urges the government to affect change where it needs to do more, especially in expanding space for political dialogue and competition, and to take steps toward a democratic transition of power.

Since the genocide, Rwanda's progress in the fields of health and development has been dramatic, and we have been a proud partner in this process. Over the last decade child mortality has been reduced by two-thirds, and life expectancy has risen from 49 years in 1995 to 64.5 in 2016. HIV/AIDS prevalence among adults has dropped from 4.7% to 3.1% in the same time period. With support from the President's Emergency Plan for AIDS Relief (PEPFAR), the Government of Rwanda has also reduced HIV transmission to newborns to just two percent.

Likewise, economic growth and opportunity have been important aspects of our partnership with Rwanda for over 20 years. From 2000 to 2015, Rwanda's economic growth averaged between 7 and 8 percent, and Rwanda currently ranks

56th out of 190 countries in the World Bank's Ease of Doing Business Index – the second-highest in Africa. Rwanda has become a model in leveraging development assistance into concrete results for its people and has reduced its dependence on foreign assistance by more than half in the last decade.

Rwanda is also a major contributor to regional peace and security. It is the fifth-largest contributor of peacekeepers in the world – remarkable for a country of just under 12 million people. Rwandan troops are regionally respected and disciplined, and they have participated in UN peacekeeping operations in the Central African Republic, Sudan, Haiti, and Mali, among others. In South Sudan, Rwanda recently deployed additional peacekeeping troops as part of the UN's Regional Protection Force. Rwanda is a priority partner in the Africa Peacekeeping Rapid Response Partnership (APRRP) and has been a leader in reforming the African Union so that it is better prepared to resolve regional conflicts. President Kagame will take over the rotating chairmanship of the AU in January 2018 for the following year.

Despite these positive areas, we continue to have serious concerns about weak democratic institutions, freedom of speech, and respect for human rights in Rwanda. There have been several important developments since this Subcommittee's last similarly-themed hearing on Rwanda in May 2015.

In December 2015, Rwandan voters approved a package of constitutional amendments including one that enabled President Kagame to stay in power beyond the two-term limit contained in Rwanda's constitution. In the run-up to that decision, we engaged in extensive public and private diplomacy, urging President Kagame to honor the commitment he had made to respect term limits when he first assumed office. The constitutional amendments allowed President Kagame, who has been in office since 2000, to run for a third term, which he has since done (and won). He could potentially stay in office until 2034, when he will turn 77 years old. Immediately after the referendum's passage, we publicly expressed deep disappointment with President Kagame's decision. We continue to publicly and privately emphasize our conviction that constitutional transitions of power are essential for strong democracies everywhere, and that efforts by incumbents to change rules to stay in power weaken democratic institutions and undermine long-term stability.

The August 4 presidential elections illustrate that democracy in Rwanda remains far from perfect. As you know, President Kagame was re-elected with an official tally of nearly 99 percent of the vote, in an election with notable shortcomings. In an August 5 statement, we said we were disturbed by the voting irregularities we observed and reiterated long-standing concerns over the integrity of the vote-counting process. Three aspiring candidates were disqualified before the election, and we expressed concern with the lack of transparency in that process. As we noted in our statement, we hope that these concerns will be addressed before the 2018 parliamentary elections.

Compared to the previous presidential elections in 2010, however, we noted some progress. This was the first election in which the Democratic Green Party, the main registered opposition party in Rwanda, was allowed to participate. The Rwandan media also reported on the harassment of some opposition candidates, and government officials took action to address those complaints – in some cases by arresting local officials.

Since the election, Rwandan authorities have targeted several political opposition figures for questioning or arrest. We are concerned by and are following closely the case of Diane Rwigara, one of the three disqualified presidential aspirants. Police raided her home on August 29 and arrested Ms. Rwigara and two of her family members on September 23. We understand the Rwandan authorities have until September 28 to press charges. In addition, we are also following the arrests of at least ten officials and members of an unregistered opposition party earlier this month. These cases suggest that tight restrictions remain on political competition and critics of the ruling party.

Other serious human rights violations we have cited in our reports to Congress include arbitrary or unlawful killings; security forces' disregard for the rule of law; restrictions on civil society organizations; and government interference with the press. Over the years, Rwandans have reported to us the disappearance and suspected deaths of family members at the hands of Rwandan security services. NGOs critical of the government are routinely denied registration to operate in the country. Government officials have also questioned, threatened, and arrested journalists who expressed critical views on sensitive topics. The government has used laws criminalizing genocide ideology and divisionism, along with national security provisions, to suppress dissent, prosecute journalists, and pressure human rights groups to refrain from investigating and reporting on their findings.

The Administration continues to take action to address the human rights situation in Rwanda:

- In March 2017, our Ambassador in Kigali initiated a quarterly high-level dialogue with the government on civil society and media freedom issues.

- USAID supports a number of targeted activities to promote the rule of law, access to justice, and the responsible growth of civil society and the media.
- Some areas where we continue to work include strengthening local NGO capacity to engage in policy making, improvements to laws governing NGOs, increasing the capacity and skills of the media to provide independent and impartial information, and skills training for judges.
- Rwanda benefits from the African Growth and Opportunity Act (AGOA), and we have raised concerns to the Rwandan government regarding harassment of political opposition leaders and NGOs as well as restrictions on media freedom within the context of AGOA's eligibility criteria.
- We are responding to Rwanda's request for help to combat trafficking in persons, including by improving prosecutorial skills and closing gaps in investigative capacity.
- Over the last decade we have worked closely with the Rwandan government, civil society, and the private sector to combat child labor. Thanks to our partnership, approximately 5,000 children were removed from child labor in Rwanda's tea-growing districts between 2015 and 2017 alone.

I would also like to note some good news with respect to human rights and governance in Rwanda. The Government of Rwanda holds public officials accountable for corrupt practices, including through prosecution. Rwanda has also prioritized the fight against gender-based violence and generally respects the rights of LGBTI persons. Women leaders are promoted, as evidenced by the fact that 63 percent of Parliament members and 40 percent of cabinet officials are female.

Human rights are part and parcel of our ongoing dialogue at all levels of the Rwandan government. Our consistent message remains that allowing opposition figures, journalists, and civil society to contribute to Rwanda's future is crucial to building the knowledge-based economy the government seeks to foster. This includes ensuring freedom of expression, press freedoms, and the ability of citizens to criticize the government and ruling party without fear of threats, violence, or intimidation.

From private engagement to public statements, we have raised and will continue to raise these issues – not just because it is the right thing to do, but because we firmly believe that Rwanda's ability to sustain the gains achieved over the last 23 years depends on building an inclusive society that protects the rights of all of its citizens.

The government and people of Rwanda have reasons to be hopeful as the country continues to build a brighter future linked to peace and economic development. The United States will continue to work in partnership with all Rwandans to support progress in security and development, and to strengthen transparent democratic institutions that welcome criticism and embrace diverse views.

Thank you, and I look forward to your questions.

Mr. SMITH. Thank you so much, Mr. Ambassador.

Let me begin by asking, did you, did the department, consider the elections to be free, fair, and transparent? You note that there is some progress.

You note that the Democratic Green Party, which got less than 1 percent—I presume far less than that in the election—rather than the other parties that might have had a more robust showing on election day, as some progress and you also point out that Rwandan media—you don't say whether or not we independently verified it—reported on harassment of some opposition candidates and that government officials took action to address those complaints.

Is that all true or is it just something that was in the local papers? Because you did point out in the next paragraph, since the election Rwandan authorities have targeted—what a word, targeted—several political opposition figures for questioning or arrest.

So those who weren't happy with the results couldn't participate the way they ought to have been able to and now get further retaliation after the election. I don't see why that is progress.

Mr. YAMAMOTO. Thank you, Mr.—thank you, Mr. Chairman.

So our relationship with Rwanda is one of a mixed relationship on the issue of democratic concerns and human rights issues.

But if we look at one issue—area is if the elections were completely free, open, fair, and transparent in a U.S. context would President Kagame win that election and the answer is he has——

Mr. SMITH. I don't think that is the question to ask. I think it should be whether or not the process was free, fair, and transparent and then let the people decide.

Mr. YAMAMOTO. Right. So after the Presidential elections we had made a statement saying that we noted irregularities in the process and that is an issue that we had raised with the government and also looked at ways in which we could work with the Government of Rwanda to improve the process in the elections.

Let me also state that one positive point for the electoral process since 2010 is that we did have the registration of the Democratic Green Party and also the first debate—political debate for the presidency.

Mr. SMITH. But his numbers, obviously—President Kagame's—have gone up to the point where they are almost 100 percent so any sense that things are trending toward more openness, transparency, would you be able to say here and now that it was a free and fair election? Yes or no?

Mr. YAMAMOTO. And the answer is more complex and the issue is that in our statement that we had stated that we had concerns with the process of the elections because of the irregularities that we noted and——

Mr. SMITH. Like, what were the irregularities?

Mr. YAMAMOTO. The irregularities concerned the process and procedures and the issue of having 98.9 percent of the vote, that in itself denotes or relates to information of irregularities.

Mr. SMITH. And candidates were excluded from participation in an arbitrary and capricious manner? Yes?

Mr. YAMAMOTO. Yes.

Mr. SMITH. Why can't we just simply say it wasn't free, it wasn't fair, wasn't transparent?

Mr. YAMAMOTO. That the—because on the overall issues that we noted the irregularities and we noticed good points and bad points, and so there is a process.

And what we hope to achieve in our overall relationship with Rwanda is that this is a reliable partnership and that we want to move it in a forward posture and that is what——

Mr. SMITH. I agree on behalf of the people we should do everything we can health wise, and everything to be of assistance, even with dictatorships.

But I don't think we should look askance and not call it for what it is. If it is a sham election we ought to call it a sham election. You can't say that?

Mr. YAMAMOTO. And we agree with you. We agree with you 100 percent.

Mr. SMITH. That it is a sham election or——

Mr. YAMAMOTO. That we look at elections and judge it by the standards of a free, fair, transparent election process and when there are irregularities we will call it out and that is what we did in August.

Mr. SMITH. But at the end of the day, a judgment has to be made based on the evidence. But you cannot or will not make the decision that it was not free, not fair, and not transparent.

Mr. YAMAMOTO. It was not a transparent process. I mean, it was not a—irregularities in the process of the election.

Mr. SMITH. At the end of the day, was it free and fair? No? Yes?

Mr. YAMAMOTO. Again, Mr. Chairman, it becomes a very complex process.

Mr. SMITH. Okay. I am not sure why you can't make a judgment. It is disappointing.

Human Rights Watch has documented that poor people—critics of government decisions regarding land disputes and suspected petty criminals have been arbitrarily arrested, held in illegal detention centers, and in some cases executed, forcefully disappeared, tortured, and mistreated. These tactics ensure that citizens are afraid to speak out against the government," and they go through what you would call one irregularity after another. Again, I don't know why the judgment can't be made that this was not a free and fair election.

Amnesty International points out in their comments quite extensively that the Rwandan Government continues to suppress the independence and freedom of the media. Numerous journalists have been imprisoned, harassed, and even killed while many more have fled into exile over the years. Then they give specific examples on that.

These actions mirror previous media crackdowns. Is there a media crackdown? Was there before the election, during the election, and after the election?

Mr. YAMAMOTO. Let me go to your first question, Mr. Chairman.

So first is on the voting and the vote count irregularities that we observed on the August 4th Presidential elections. We are not able—we are unable to assess this election as free and fair so that is our original statement.

We have communicated our observations and assessment to the Rwandan Government. On the issues of human rights abuse during the procedures and process of the elections before, during, and after, we are concerned with any reports of human rights.

We have started, through our Ambassador, through our Embassy, engaging with the government at all levels on these issues and we express our concerns.

Mr. SMITH. And, again, if I could, with all due respect, Mr. Ambassador, we have had human rights dialogues in places like Vietnam for years.

They have been a cul-de-sac where people meet, nothing happens—a venting of disagreements—and then they are used as an excuse for not calling out Vietnam for its egregious abuses whether it be as a CPC country or as a violator with regards to trafficking.

The dialogues are important but they can't be a substitute for calling it the way it is in a forum like this or anywhere else, particularly after the election.

Ninety-nine percent. One party is given the green light, which was destined to lose massively. I don't see that as progress when so many others were disqualified.

So I would take issue with your assessment of some progress. I think, if anything, it is regression, given his even better outcome that he had in the polls.

Amnesty International and Human Rights Watch documented just how brutal this was.

As a matter of fact, Amnesty International said in their testimony during the 23 years that the Rwandan Patriotic Front has ruled the country there has been an unwavering often brutal campaign against government critics and human rights defenders.

This campaign has included a tax on political opposition members including arrest, detention, disappearance and killings, restrictions on the media, and activities of civil society and the creation of a climate of fear.

And now, as you have testified, since the election Rwanda authorities have targeted several political opposition figures for questioning or arrest. I mean, he's not even satisfied that he got his outcome. Now he has to go after them and crush them now.

Mr. YAMAMOTO. You know, as I said, Mr. Chairman, that the relationship is complex but it is also a mixed record and I know your position and we respect it and do emphasize that we, as the government, are committed to looking at the concerns that you have raised today and that we have raised them as well directly with the government, and we continue to raise them and to work with them to improve those areas where we believe that we can make a difference.

And in some areas the Rwandan Government has made dramatic increases from child labor issues to allowing opposition parties to debates to accepting recommendations from the peer group under the U.N. operations and to look at. So we note that there is progress but there are, obviously, areas that we still need to work on and we are doing that.

Mr. SMITH. Let me ask you one final question. Major Robert Higiro, obviously, testified before. He is here today, and he was not believed at first by the State Department and I know you have to do your due diligence and I deeply respect that. My understanding is that you came to the conclusion that he had a credible case when he came forward and said that he was offered money—$1 million—to assassinate a general and a colonel who had fled Rwanda to South Africa.

In his testimony today, he thanks America profusely. He had a death threat against him when he was living in Belgium and now has come to the United States.

He points out in his testimony that members of the opposition parties and the media continue to disappear. Present tense—not past tense, present tense.

How do you assess his revelations and this idea that members of the opposition parties and media continue to disappear?

Mr. YAMAMOTO. You know, our position remains very clear. We have received the book from Mr. Higiro and I will diligently read that in detail.

But, again, we remain concerned by the history of Rwanda's treatment of opposition people and the issues that were raised by Mr. Higiro and others, those are issues and concerns that we will pursue and follow and follow up on.

And, again, on the other side, for the Rwandan side, is we continue to help Rwanda build strong democratic institutions and those—that is really fundamentally the bottom line is to build those institutions which can address those concerns that we have raised and continue to raise and those are issues that we share with you, Mr. Chairman.

Mr. SMITH. But, again, on those institutions, you're talking about an electoral process that is egregiously flawed, where is the success in building that institution? It just facilitates a 99 percent vote.

Mr. YAMAMOTO. We have faith and confidence that through these—through our efforts that we will be able to work with this government and also others because we do see positive developments and through, I think——

Mr. SMITH. Do you see a change of attitude on the part of President Kagame?

Mr. YAMAMOTO. I think that in certain areas we have seen improvement. In other areas, we see——

Mr. SMITH. He will be there until 2034, right?

Mr. YAMAMOTO. Under the changes in the constitution if he gets elected two more times, sure.

Ms. BASS. Thank you.

Mr. Ambassador, what role, if any, should the U.S. play in supporting Rwanda's stability and efforts to improve the quality of lives of Rwandan citizens and what role should Congress play?

Mr. YAMAMOTO. First of all, we extend our deep appreciation to you, Madam Congresswoman, and to you, Mr. Chairman, for all the efforts and issues you have raised to highlight the concerns that you have on Africa but also on a wide range of issues.

So the stability of not just Rwanda but of the region and the states is critical not only to the security of that area but also stability and concern for the entire continent, and also it goes into our national strategic interest.

So let me say to your question is what is it that we would like to achieve? We would like to see a stable democratic country which respects the rights of the citizens, respects the rights and freedoms of a free press and that it helps with the education opportunities and opportunities in general of its people.

Ms. BASS. So what are we doing in that regard, especially in regard to democracy and governance?

Mr. YAMAMOTO. To that end, we have several USAID programs. I think our development and assistance and assistance overall is about $159 million a year.

On the one hand, on security side, the Rwandans have remained extremely supportive and a very good partner in peacekeeping operations and troops.

On the side of health care, you cited, Madam Congresswoman, of the tremendous changes that they have made through health care, through HIV/AIDS progress.

Ms. BASS. Yes.

Mr. YAMAMOTO And also on women playing a constructive role in society, and also girls education and women entrepreneurs. Those are areas that are positive and really stand as symbol for other countries as well.

Ms. BASS. So in terms of our democracy and governance?

Mr. YAMAMOTO. And our democracy and governance is to create strong institutions and, again——

Ms. BASS. We have specific programs. I worry about this specific area because I know in the proposed cuts, if I am not mistaken, this takes a major hit.

Mr. YAMAMOTO. And that does. Rwanda's democratic institutions are still developing. We believe that and we need to focus more on creating those strong institutions which can carry between this President and to the next President and also for successive leaderships.

That is what we want to achieve and I think those are the objectives and goals that we are committed to along with our NGO partners and also our discussions with the Government of Rwanda.

Ms. BASS. So to what extent is Rwanda's continued development progress contingent on continued donor aid or how much is independent?

Mr. YAMAMOTO. In other words, to tie assistance to benchmarks for development and—so on health care you can't set—the benchmark is progress and that progress is clear and evident——

Ms. BASS. Right.

Mr. YAMAMOTO [continuing]. From livelihood and length of life expectancy and health care and HIV/AIDS. When you talk about development and human rights and democratic values, we have laws in place from our AGOA trading investments.

There is an aspect on democracy and human rights. As you know, we have written letters of warning to the government on human rights issues.

On the other issue is we have the Child Soldier Protection Act (CSPA) law and then the other law that the Congress has passed on the 2017 Appropriations Act.

So those are areas that we look at and say that these are areas that we can hold the Government of Rwanda accountable. So, for instance, we had suspended FMF—foreign military financing. We had suspended IMET—military education. And, really, this is——

Ms. BASS. What about direct military assistance?

Mr. YAMAMOTO. And direct military. We had not——

Ms. BASS. We suspended it. We suspended education and we suspended——

Mr. YAMAMOTO. The FMF. Right. But in this past year we have not renewed FMF but we have renewed—we have continued with IMET because really in that——

Ms. BASS. What did you say IMET was again?

Mr. YAMAMOTO. International Military Education Training program.

Ms. BASS. Uh-huh.

Mr. YAMAMOTO. So the IMET program really is, in many ways, our—it is in our national interest as well because by taking Rwandan troops and officers to the United States——

Ms. BASS. Yes.

Mr. YAMAMOTO [continuing]. To give them an education on human rights, that makes them a better officer.

Ms. BASS. Thank you.

Mr. SMITH. Thank you very much, Ms. Bass.

Just one final question. The State Department has long declined to accept the various U.N. reports of Rwandan involvement in the smuggling of resources from the Democratic Republic of the Congo or its support for militia inside the country. What is the view of the department today? There are two reports on that.

Mr. YAMAMOTO. So we—so we continue monitoring the conflict minerals in the Congo, which countries and operations are developing, from foreign countries to regional states, et cetera, and Rwanda has been in—in that area have been very supportive, passing laws to monitor the conflict minerals and we have been working with the Rwandan Government to reinforce those laws and also to criminalize any individuals who has engaged in illegal or illicit trading.

Mr. SMITH. And, again, getting back, briefly, to Robert Higiro, does the State Department believe him to be credible?

Mr. YAMAMOTO. I respect Mr. Higiro very much. I think the position he held as an advisor to President Kagame and the words that he presents in his testimony as the next witness I stand ready to listen to what he is going to present and the concerns of human rights, et cetera, we will continue to look into those issues.

Mr. SMITH. Now, this is Major Robert Higiro, who, again, was offered $1 million to kill. So you believe he's credible?

Mr. YAMAMOTO. I respect him as an individual who has had a senior position in the government and his issues of human rights abuse or other concerns is an issue that we will look into and we will work with him.

Mr. SMITH. Because David Himbara was very high up with the government but it is the major who was offered this incentive to murder people. So you believe they are both credible?

Mr. YAMAMOTO. So let me—we will stand and listen to his testimony today and we will have other—further conversations later with him.

Mr. SMITH. Thank you very much, Mr. Ambassador.

Mr. YAMAMOTO. And thank you, Mr. Chairman and Madam Congresswoman——

Mr. SMITH. Thank you.

Mr. YAMAMOTO [continuing]. Not only for having this hearing but also for your concern, and we remain committed to working with you because I think we share a very commonality in what we want to achieve.

Thank you very much.

Mr. SMITH. Thank you so very much, Mr. Ambassador.

I'd like to now invite to the witness table, first beginning with David Himbara, who is coordinator for Canada at Democracy in Rwanda Now.

As a former close aide to President Paul Kagame, Mr. Himbara held a leading role focused on socioeconomic development in Rwanda. Tasked with improving national competitiveness, he spearheaded efforts that ultimately improved Rwanda's ranking in the World Bank's annual Doing Business Report. He's an author and his latest book is "Kagame's Killing Fields."

Next, we will hear from Robert Higiro, who is coordinator for the United States at Democracy in Rwanda Now. Prior to moving to the United States, he served as a major in the Rwandan Defense Force.

He was part of the force that took control of Kigali in 1994 that toppled the then-Hutu government and helped bring an end to the genocide in Rwanda.

After his decommission, he was tasked by the Rwandan Government with assassinating officials and dissidents that fell out of favor with the Kagame regime. Instead of following those orders, Major Higiro went to the press and unveiled the plot at great risk to himself. It led to his being insecure in Belgium and the need for him to move to the United States for his own personal security.

We will then hear from Mr. Mike Jobbins, who serves as the Africa Program's manager for Search for Common Ground. He previously worked in Search for Common Ground field programs in the DRC in Burundi where he supported the startup and management projects on SGBV prevention, refugee reintegration, security sector reform, and post-war governance.

Mr. Jobbins has led field missions in humanitarian and emergency settings in North Katanga, North Kivu, Equateur provinces of the DRC. He also testified previously before this subcommittee.

And then we will hear from Adotei Akwei, who serves in the government relations office for Amnesty International. Mr. Adotei is a political analyst and experienced advocate and campaigner, a U.S. foreign security policy advisor as well as an advocate for rights-based approach to ending poverty with field experience in Africa as well as in Asia.

He is also a regular spokesman for Amnesty International USA, for print, radio, and television in the United States, Europe, and Africa and he, too, is welcome back to our committee.

Mr. David Himbara, if you would begin.

STATEMENT OF MR. DAVID HIMBARA, COORDINATOR FOR CANADA, DEMOCRACY IN RWANDA NOW

Mr. HIMBARA. Chairman Smith, Ranking Member Karen Bass, ladies and gentlemen, I thank you very much indeed for giving me—giving me the opportunity to talk about democracy and human rights in Rwanda.

I would like to talk about three things. First, I want to give the context of the recent elections. Then number two, I want to talk about the elections themselves, and then number three, I wish to talk about post-elections.

The context of the elections in Rwanda was the constitutional amendment made in 2015. The constitutional amendment did two things. One, it removed a very, very important part of the previous constitution which said that, I quote, "under no circumstances should President of Rwanda serve more than two 7-year terms." Why was this in the original constitution?

It was in the original constitution because, historically, since independence, each leader in Rwanda has come through violence and then was removed by violence, and each of those Presidents— and the main ones have been three—in their terms each one managed to win elections by 98 percent. So this is not just a Kagame issue. All of them.

And, of course, as I said, they became a power unto themselves and we have not had any peaceful transfer of power in Rwanda.

So that was the importance of that clause that under no circumstances. This is what was removed by the amendment so now President Kagame can stay in power until 2034.

Now, there was something even worse than that. There is something even worse than that in the amendment. In the new constitution they inserted what we call Article 114 and it is called exemption from prosecution for a former head of state.

The article reads, "A former President of the republic cannot be prosecuted for treason or serious and deliberate violation of the constitution when no legal proceedings in respect of that offense were brought against him while in office."

Well, of course, it cannot be brought against him while he's in office because he has immunity. So Kagame has immunized himself even after he leaves power.

This article basically gives him license to commit any crimes without any consequences. How do we explain this? By the way, incidentally, I must say with a bit of sick humor these amendments are being made by the women majority of Parliament. These are women in the majority of Parliament at work.

So the numbers of women is great but the quality of work they do is rubber stamping the worst possible. Okay.

So why is he doing this? We already know that even to come here in the United States Kagame had to be given immunity.

The Obama administration asserted immunity for him because there are already cases about the alleged role in the shooting down of the previous President. This is the background behind this.

But we also know that currently in the International Court of Justice there is a quote by Congo that accuses Kagame the crime of killing 3.5 million people. Rwanda and Uganda were both taken to this court.

Uganda pleaded its case and lost and is paying reparations. Rwanda denied jurisdiction of the court.

So this case won't disappear. It is sitting in there somewhere. So that is the context. That is the context.

Then the elections themselves—I don't have to say much because a lot was covered—99 percent out of 96 voter turnout. This begins now to take us closer to the situation of North Korea. But, incidentally, this clause that frees Kagame from any prosecution, I have looked at the worst dictatorships. I have not found any such protection.

Now, the elections themselves—I want to quote the British Ambassador. The British Ambassador was among the observers of the elections so I quote him.

He says that, "Along with other international observers, I personally saw irregularities with the counting of ballots and voter tabulation."

And then he concludes, "We are concerned by the arrests and it is concerning to see the targeting of opposition figures." This is the British Ambassador in Rwanda.

So I really don't have much to say but now let me talk about post-elections. Post-election is now revenge. It is a period of revenge. It is a revenge big time, and revenge has a single in particular—Diane Shima Rwigara.

Why her? Why her? There are a number of reasons why her. First of all, she is the one who dared to raise issues of democracy, issues of human rights, issues of moral corruption, and by moral corruption she was saying that even in this economic miracle people talk about the ruling party itself has accumulated so much wealth that its conglomerate, Crystal Ventures, is now worth $500 million while the same government punishes and destroys other businesses.

Rwigara's own father was killed 2 years ago in a serious accident. When the family protested, the government moved on and demolished their hotel.

A month ago, another hotel, a competitor to the ruling party—Tower Hotel—was demolished in broad daylight. Just 2 days ago, the leading Rwandan businessman, Tribert Rujugiro Ayabatwa, his $20 million Union Trade Center was seized and auctioned for $8 million.

So I guess I am running out of time. I see some signals there.

So in conclusion, what we have here is a very costly experiment. Even those people who talk about the good things—the women in parliament—by the way, those women are—no one has voted. That Parliament is a list compiled by the ruling party—the senators, half of them appointed.

Don't confuse the senators in Rwanda with the senators in United States or Congress people. No. These are lists—party lists. Those who are not elected by the President, they are elected by people he has appointed in other institutions.

Business success, absolutely not. Yes, if we talk about the President traveling in a $60 million plane rented from his own business at the taxpayers' cost, if that is success—I don't think so.

So what should the United States be doing? I think the United States, in my view, has overcompensated. During the Clinton years during genocide, the government stood by while terrible crimes were committed.

Then comes Kagame. So now we have gone overboard. He can do no wrong. I think that it is time that we take a closer look. We are not asking by any means to say stop health support or stop education. No. But the same military that you are supporting is the same military that is killing its own people.

So what is good with a military that is doing great in the full when it is mowing down people in Rwanda and Congo? There is a problem there.

I will simply say this. But first of all, I conclude by thanking you very much for having this hearing but also let me thank the Congress because I believe that in the budget law of 2017 there is a clause in there that says that for any government in the Great Lakes region to receive military support the State Department must verify if this government—if any government is causing havoc—they are not using those words—is causing havoc in the neighborhood.

So I think you ought to hold your State Department accountable to see if they are doing this because we know for sure that causing havoc in Burundi or in Congo has not stopped, which I am sure my colleague here will say more about.

I thank you so much for giving me a few minutes to talk.

[The prepared statement of Mr. Himbara follows:]

Testimony of David Himbara, House Foreign Affairs Committee Subcommittee on African Affairs,

September 27, 2017

RWANDA: DEMOCRACY THWARTED

Chairman Chris Smith, Ranking Member Karen Bass, and Members of the Committee:

Thank you very much indeed for providing me with the opportunity to address the Committee on democracy and human rights in my country, Rwanda. Let me begin my testimony with the August 2017 presidential election won by the incumbent President Paul Kagame, by a purported 99% in voter turnout of 98%. Among those unconvinced by this extraordinary result were the main bilateral financiers of the Kagame regime – namely, the United States and the United Kingdom. For the United States, the State Department said that it was "concerned by the lack of transparency in determining the eligibility of prospective candidates." The State Department added that **"we are disturbed by irregularities observed during voting and reiterate long-standing concerns over the integrity of the vote-tabulation process."**[1] The United Kingdom was even direct. The British High Commissioner in Rwanda stated that he was concerned by **"the lack of clarity in the registration process for candidates which appear to have made it impossible for certain credible candidates to register."** He further stated that **"along with other international observers, I personally saw irregularities with the counting of ballots and vote tabulation."** He concluded that he was "concerned by the arrests" in recent weeks and that **"It is concerning to see the targeting of opposition figures."**[2]

Let me illustrate what the American and British governments are saying with the story of Diane Shima Rwigara. This story best demonstrates how the Rwandan state, under President Paul Kagame's rule, is determined to stamp out democracy and its advocates. But this account is also about courage, audacity, and determination to confront brute power at personal risk.

---

[1] US State Department, "Presidential Election in Rwanda," August 5, 2017, https://www.state.gov/r/pa/prs/ps/2017/08/273206.htm

[2] William Gelling, the UK High Commissioner to Rwanda and Burundi, "International Day of Democracy," September 15, 2017, https://www.gov.uk/government/speeches/international-day-of-democracy

The Diane Rwigara story began in May 2017 when she announced plans to seek the Rwandan presidency. Her motivation to enter politics was to fight for democracy, free speech, justice, poverty and moral corruption. She asserted that she would no longer live in fear of the ruling party's violence that affects all Rwandans. Diane denounced politicians in Rwanda and Africa that change constitutions to cling to power. She raised the issue of rulers living like kings and queens while most Rwandans live in mass poverty. She criticized Kagame and his ruling Rwandan Patriotic Front for acquiring a US$500 million business empire, Crystal Venture, based on cronyism, while terrorizing genuine businesspeople.

Diane Rwigara knew what she was talking about. Two years earlier her own father had died in a mysterious car accident. When her family demanded an official investigation, the government demolished the family's hotel. Diane had also observed many cases whereby business persons lost their assets on Kagame's orders. One such case is Tribert Rujugiro's US$20 million shopping mall, which was illegally seized by Kagame.

Diana's audacity was unthinkable in Kagame's Rwanda. Most of her compatriots were stunned by her courage. The regime hit back by denying her the right to compete for high office.

But Diane Rwigara would not be silenced. She persisted with her peaceful fight for democracy and human rights. After being blocked for competing for the presidency, she launched a democracy movement. She formed a "People Salvation Movement" with a goal of sensitizing Rwandans about their rights. She would also continue to criticize the human rights abuses of the ruling party, the Rwanda Patriotic Front (RPF).

Kagame would have none of it. After angrily referring to Diane Rwigara as "a failed presidential candidate" who does not have immunity from prosecution, the Rwandan security forces raided the Rwigara home. She was locked up in her house along with her entire family for nearly a month. Each day Diane, her mother, and sister would be dragged to Rwanda intelligence headquarters for questioning for over 15 hours. Then on September 24, 2017, Diane, her mother Adeline, and her sister Anne, were arrested. They were charged with "offences against state security and other offences."

That sums up the political environment in Rwanda. There is no space for democracy or human rights in Rwanda. In prison, Diane Rwigara will join others who tried to challenge

Kagame's dictatorship. She will find people like Victoire Ingabire Umuhoza. She will find Deo Mushayidi, and many known and unknown political activists. Diane will find families of former intelligence chief, Patrick Karegeya, who was assassinated in South Africa three years ago. She will find families of former army chief of staff, Kayumba Nyamwasa, who has survived four assassination attempts. Democracy in Rwanda is very problematic. The 2015 amendment to the Rwandan constitutional made matters worse by giving a green light to incumbent head of state to commit crimes and get away with it. Article 114 on the "Exemption from prosecution for a former president of the Republic" asserts:

> "A former President of the Republic *cannot be prosecuted for treason or serious and deliberate violation of the Constitution* when no legal proceedings in respect of that offence were brought against him or her while in office."[3]

Meanwhile the 2015 Rwandan constitution permits Kagame to stay in power until 2034.

What should the United States do to assist the people of Rwanda? As the top foreign aid-donor to Rwanda at $128 million in 2016,[4] United States can at least isolate Kagame and his regime. The US State Department rightly condemned the August 2017 flawed elections that extended Kagame's rule. This is not enough. The United States should do more than merely calling Kagame out on his repression of the Rwandan people. The US should cut off nonessential support to Kagame such as military aid. Further, we call upon the American government to pressure the Kagame regime to free the Rwigara family and other political prisoners immediately. After all, one of the Rwigaras, Anne, is an American citizen.

I thank you for your kind attention.

[3] Republic of Rwanda, "Constitution of Rwanda, 2015,"
http://www.minijust.gov.rw/fileadmin/Law_and_Regulations/Official_Gazette_no_Special_of_24.12.2015__2__1_.pdf
[4] USAID, "The History of USAID/Rwanda," https://www.usaid.gov/history-usaidrwanda

Mr. SMITH. Mr. Himbara, thank you so very much for your testimony.

I would like to now recognize Robert Higiro.

STATEMENT OF MAJOR ROBERT HIGIRO, RWANDA DEFENSE FORCE, RETIRED, COORDINATOR FOR THE UNITED STATES, DEMOCRACY IN RWANDA NOW

Major HIGIRO. Chairman Smith, Ranking Member Bass, members of the subcommittee, ladies and gentlemen, good afternoon.

I thank you for giving me the opportunity to give testimony on democracy and human rights in Rwanda. I wish to give evidence. My purpose today is to give evidence to the fact that democracy in Rwanda is impossible because of the environment that exists in the country right now. The commander-in-chief of the Rwandan security forces are part of the problem. Their purpose is not to provide security, but, rather to kill Rwandans and cause chaos in the region.

Let me begin with President Kagame himself. He is on the record after the 2016 State Department report when they are concerned by disappearances saying, those who talk about disappearances are wasting time. As he puts it, "We will shoot them, if possible, in broad daylight." That is the President saying it; I am just quoting him. It is not my words; it is his words. We have seen the follow-up of his senior commanders, brigade commanders, division commanders, echoing the same tone, especially in the western region.

In the 2016 State Department's Human Rights Report, it gives the most recent relatives in Rwanda. An increasing number of people have disappeared or have been reported missing since May 2015. That is since our previous hearing. Many of the cases occurred in Rubavu district in the Western Province. According to Human Rights Watch reports, most of these people were detained by Rwanda Defence Forces, and we believe that they are in military custody. Witnesses saw some of the local authorities participating in this activity. One was the executive Secretary in Rubavu district by the name of Mugisha. He was seen taking part in those who were forcibly being kidnapped together with security agents. Imam Mohamed Mugemangango was shot and killed while in custody. At least half a dozen of people have been murdered by the security forces while in prison.

Extrajudicial killings recently increased as the security forces cleared the capital of Kigali and major towns of poor people, unemployed, and the homeless. Authorities are rounding up poor people and arbitrarily detaining them in transit centers. They have transit centers across the country. In its 2017 report, Human Rights Watch proved chilling details of extrajudicial killing of 37 Rwandans suspected of petty offenses such as stealing bananas or a car or a motorcycle in the Western Province. That was between July 2016 and 2017. Soldiers have continued to arrest and shoot most of the victims in what appears to be an officially-sanctioned strategy by the government.

The claims by the state against Rwandans never stop, and this includes dissidents, those inside the country, and they go as far as Europe. That is why I am here. I try to travel as far as possible; they still come for you. We will get a chance to elaborate on that.

Rwanda's destabilization of neighboring countries has also not stopped, particularly in the Democratic Republic of Congo and Burundi. In 2013 in DRC, Rwanda disarmed over 770 M23 Congolese rebel combatants it had previously sponsored to take over the eastern part of the DRC. After the defeat of M23, over 770 crossed into Rwanda, the same number, and were detained in Ngoma. According to the 2016 State Department report, the same number mysteriously vanished. There can be no doubt about their role; they are Rwanda's proxy army used to destabilize the neighbors.

In the case of Burundi, Rwanda stands accused of recruiting Burundian refugees into the armed groups who seek to overthrow the government of President Pierre Nkurunziza. In its report, "Asylum Betrayed: Recruitment of Burundian Refugees in Rwanda," the Refugees International rebuked Rwanda in the following terms: "The Rwandan Government must act at once to ensure the civilian and humanitarian character of asylum and protected refugees from recruitment by non-state armed actors. To that end, it must ensure that all efforts to recruit Burundian refugees into armed groups— whether on or emanating from Rwandan territory, and whether committed by Burundian or Rwandan nationals—cease immediately." That was Refugees International. "Rwanda must also affirm publicly that the recruitment of refugees into non-state armed groups on its territory is a violation of international and Rwandan law."

Mr. Chairman, I can't repeat what has been said, whether it is on the peace prospect or the corruption. That is why I want to conclude by thanking you once again for conducting this congressional hearing on Rwanda. We trust that the United States, being the main donor to Rwanda, will make its support conditional to ending terror on its own people and the region.

Thank you very much.

[The prepared statement of Major Higiro follows:]

Testimony of Major, Robert Higiro: Subcommittee on Africa, Global Health, Global Human Rights, and International Organizations
U.S. House of Representatives
Sept, 27th 2017.

Chairman Smith, Ranking Member Bass, Members of the Subcommittee, Ladies and Gentlemen. Good afternoon.

Thank you very much for inviting me here once again, as I had the privilege of addressing you in May 2015. I want to thank you for what the government of the United States did for me after I appeared before this Committee two years ago. In my 2015 testimony, I gave details of how, after serving as a major in the Rwandan military, the Rwandan intelligence had offered me US$1 million to assassinate General Kayumba Nyamwasa and Colonel Patrick Karegeya who had fled Rwanda to South Africa. The repression of critical voices inside Rwanda, dissidents and real or perceived critics outside the country in neighboring Uganda, Tanzania and Kenya, South Africa and Europe have been victims of attacks and threats. In connection with my testimony of 2015 the United States' officials relocated me to the United States after learning that the government of Rwanda was attempting to kill me in Belgium. I have since been living in the United States and am most thankful for the generosity of the American people.

Mr Chairman, since 2015, the government of Rwanda has become increasingly authoritarian and violent. Its security forces continue to murder Rwandans and destabilize neighboring countries.

In May 2015, I mentioned the extra-judicial assassinations of Patrick Karegeya in South Africa, but also of Assinapol Rwigara, a Rwandan businessman and Dr Emmanuel Gasakure, the private cardiologist of President Kagame, both killed in Rwanda. These assassinations are linked to the corruption of the regime. President Kagame owns all businesses in the country, either through private companies held by front men or through companies belonging to the ruling party, primarily Crystal Ventures. Any individual challenging this state of affair or competing with President's Kagame business interests is eliminated. Since then the families of these men were harassed. Five members of Patrick Karegeya's family disappeared, allegedly secretly detained: Goretti Kabuto, Mutsinzi Eric, Mwine Amos, Kabanza Edward and Gashaija Jotham. Unconfirmed reports indicate that Kabanza Edward may have been killed. Recently, Diane Rwigara, who publicly opposed President Kagame and denounced these murders was arrested together with her mother and two siblings.

Members of opposition parties and the media also continue to "disappear." For example, Illuminee Iragena, a member of the unregistered United Democratic Forces (FDU)-Inkingi party, disappeared in 2015. Unconfirmed reports suggest she was killed in detention. In August 2017, the entire leadership of this FDU party vanished. Members or sympathizers of the Rwanda National Congress (RNC), the political party working outside Rwanda are systematically targeted.

The 2016 State Department's Human Rights report confirmed unlawful killings in the country. An increasing number of people have disappeared or have been reported missing since May 2015 in Rwanda. Many of the cases occurred in Rubavu district, in Western Province. According to

Human Rights Watch reports, most of these people were detained by Rwanda Defence Force (RDF) soldiers and we believe they are in military custody. Witnesses saw the executive secretary of Gisenyi sector, Honoré Mugisha, taking part in arrests of people who were forcibly kidnapped together with security agents. Imam Mohamed Mugemangango was shot and killed while he was in custody – At least half a dozen of people have been murdered by the security forces while in prison.

Extrajudicial killings recently increased as the security forces cleared the capital city of Kigali and major towns of poor people, unemployed, and the homeless. Authorities are rounding up poor people and arbitrarily detaining them in "transit centers" across the country. In its 2017 report, Human Rights Watch proved chilling details of extrajudicial killing of 37 Rwandans suspected of petty offences such as stealing bananas, a cow, or a motorcycle in Rwanda's Western Province between July 2016 and March 2017. Soldiers arbitrarily arrested and shot most of the victims, in what appears to be an officially sanctioned strategy. These killings, carried out by and with the backing of state agents, are a blatant violation of both Rwandan law and international human rights law.

Rwanda's destabilization of neighboring countries has also not stopped, particularly, in the Democratic Republic of Congo (DRC), and Burundi. In 2013 in DRC, Rwanda disarmed over 770 M23 Congolese rebel combatants it had previously sponsored to take over the eastern part of Democratic Republic of Congo. After the defeat of M23, over 770 crossed into Rwanda and were detained in Ngoma. According to the 2016 State Department, the 770 combatants mysteriously vanished. There can be no doubt about their role- they are Rwanda's proxy army used to destabilize the neighbors.

In the case of Burundi, Rwanda stand accused of recruiting Burundian refugees into the armed groups who seek to overthrow the government of President Pierre Nkurunziza. In its report, "Asylum Betrayed: Recruitment of Burundian Refugees in Rwanda", Refugees International rebuked Rwanda in the following terms: "The Rwandan government must act at once to ensure the civilian and humanitarian character of asylum and protect refugees from recruitment by non-state armed actors. To that end, it must ensure that all efforts to recruit Burundian refugees into armed groups-whether on or emanating from Rwandan territory, and whether committed by Burundian or Rwandan nationals- cease immediately. Rwanda must also affirm publicly that the recruitment of refugees into non-state armed groups on its territory is a violation of international and Rwandan law."

Mr Chairman, the Rwandan security forces pretend to defend human rights as peacekeepers in other countries, yet they kill their own people. Today, the Rwanda security forces are fractious and unstable. Many high ranking officers are detained: four military colonels, Colonel Claude Mugabo, Gishaije Emmanuel, Peter Kalimba and Emmanuel Rugazora were recently arrested and taken to unknown locations. Their Commander in chief, General. Paul Kagame is always seen wearing bulletproof vests and is surrounded by a wall of security. He openly acknowledges violence against Rwandan people. In June 2014, for instance, after the U.S State Department said it was deeply concerned by the arrests and disappearance of dozens of Rwandans, Kagame had the following to say: "Those who talk about disappearances... we will continue to arrest more suspects and if possible shoot them in broad daylight those who intend to destabilize our country". Mr. Chairman, if Rwanda's strong man is himself afraid of his own people and military, what is he afraid of? On most grounds Rwanda is back where it was in the months before the 1994 genocide. Are we going to blame ourselves again for not having taken action?

Mr Chairman, I conclude by thanking you once again for conducting this congressional hearing on Rwanda. We trust that the United States,being the main donor to Rwanda, will make its support conditional to ending terror on its own people and on the people on the region.

Mr. SMITH. Major Higiro, thank you very much for your testimony and for your insights.

I would like to now recognize Mr. Jobbins.

STATEMENT OF MR. MIKE JOBBINS, MANAGER, AFRICA PROGRAMS, SEARCH FOR COMMON GROUND

Mr. JOBBINS. Thank you. Chairman Smith, Ranking Member Bass, and guests, it is an honor to join you today, and I thank you for the work and to shine a candle to the crises facing Africa and its Great Lakes region. I have been before you before on Burundi and CAR and greatly appreciate you maintaining the attention there.

My name is Mike Jobbins, and for the last 9 years I have worked with Search for Common Ground throughout Africa and around the world. Search is a conflict transformation organization and we work to support peace, reconciliation, and inclusive governance here in America and in 44 countries around the world.

The testimony that follows is informed by my experience with Search, but the opinions are my own, and I ask that the written testimony be entered into the record.

Mr. SMITH. Without objection, so ordered.

Mr. JOBBINS. Search was founded on the philosophy that conflict is an inevitable part of human societies, and our aim is to promote the positive aspects of conflict through dialogue, inclusive decision-making, and creative thinking, while preventing the negative aspects, including violence, oppression, and humanitarian suffering.

We prioritized the Great Lakes beginning in 1995, opening our first office in Bujumbura, as the region was wracked by one of the worst periods of destructive conflict that the recent history has seen, and made a long-term commitment, expanding to Rwanda in 2006, with the aim of supporting inclusive decision-making and reconciliation efforts following the tragic genocide.

Over the past decade, Search worked with Rwanda media, government, civil society, and local communities to support reconciliation; address land disputes; build a capacity of civil society and government institutions, with a particular focus on youth and women in rural areas. And in preparing today, I was asked to speak specifically to our work in Rwanda focused on economic and social rights, particularly around land as well as on supporting reconciliation and post-conflict governance on the ground that affect ordinary Rwandans in the country. And so, my testimony will focus primarily on those topics.

To set the scene, Rwanda is the most densely populated country in Africa, as has been noted. To bring that home, it is slightly smaller than the state of Maryland with twice as many people, nearly all of whom are dependent on subsistence agriculture, and the population is growing quickly. When I started first working with Rwanda 10 years ago, there were 9 million Rwandans. Today there are 12 million. And that is 33 percent grown in just 10 years.

So, it is growing quickly and the underlying math is very clear. Rwandans needed, and still need, rapid economic diversification and growth as well a system to effectively manage land disputes and competition and the stresses that rural populations were feeling as population grows and resources became depleted.

And yet, despite the structural challenges in a dense, landlocked, and post-conflict country, Rwanda experienced a dramatic economic transformation. In the last 15 years, according to the World Bank numbers, the economy has quintupled with the GDP growing from $1.3 billion to $8.3 billion a year, and a lot of that has been driven by a transition away from a subsistence economy and commodity exports and toward greater value-added services, cognizant and relevant to sort of the stresses on rural agriculture.

Economic growth has been facilitated, as Congresswoman Bass highlighted, by a regulatory environment that supports business and entrepreneurship in line with the government's Vision 2020. At the same time, in the context of scarcity, disputes over the allocation, access, and ownership of land remain the most common cause of conflict for ordinary Rwandans. The government has tried to address this issue by adopting policies and putting in place local conflict mediators known as Abunzi. These mediators are put on the frontlines of solving serious disputes among stressed rural populations faced with large caseloads, varying degrees of training, and confronted with serious social obstacles, particularly around gender. While women are legally entitled to inherit property and, as noted, there has been a great emphasis on women's political participation, the right isn't always necessarily recognized or respected in practice, due to traditional norms and struggles that ordinary rural women have to access justice.

And so, to support alternative dispute resolution, Search partnered with the Ministry of Justice to support 4,000 Abunzi mediators, including female Abunzi, to support and train community resource people who could serve as advocates for the socioeconomic rights of marginalized groups and particularly for women, and to produce radio programming to ensure that rural residents understand land laws and policies and have the opportunity to ask questions and raise concerns, and finally, to build problem-solving skills, so that communities and families can address land conflicts themselves without referring to overstretching the justice system.

At the same time, it is clear that, given demographic pressure, agriculture in its current form will not sustain Rwanda's growing population. There has been an important focus from the government and from its international partners on developing alternative livelihoods and trying to ensure equal access to opportunities, particularly for rural youth and women to benefit from the economic transformation. But, as in all societies undergoing rapid high-technology economic change, the poorest and least educated struggle to take advantage of the new opportunities in the service-oriented, globalized, and educationally-intensive economy.

Impediments faced by Rwandans include a lack of information and access to opportunities, a lack of capital and education to seize those opportunities, and a lack of exposure to role models and examples of entrepreneurship to roll those out and take them to scale. And so, looking forward, alternative livelihoods are critical and the kinds of partnerships of the kind we have been developing with the private sector and media to help ensure that Rwandans from the lowest socioeconomic brackets have information access to take advantage of the opportunities available.

In terms of reconciliation and post-conflict governance, Rwanda's recovery from the horrific genocide 23 years ago has been held as a modern-day success story, both in reconciliation and good governance. Some of the statistics have been thrown out earlier. I would also add that Rwanda ranks 44th on Transparency International's Corruption Perceptions Index, some of the best scores of any African country.

And this has been achieved through a governance model that focuses on and prioritizes professional, results-oriented, and technocratic governance with strong central leadership in policymaking and implementation. The strong coordinating role that the central government plays across society has helped stamp out petty corruption and drive a coherent policy vision and agenda.

But Vision 2020 also establishes a vision for decentralization and ownership, local ownership, of government policy. Ordinary local officials face the difficult task in balancing the emphasis on efficiency and results with the need for the more cumbersome process of creating opportunities for citizen inputs, engagement in explaining policies to ordinary people. The best Rwandan administrators establish two-way communications with their citizens to tell and shape policy implementation, but in other circumstances citizens struggle to find a window to feed into decision-making in an environment where there is not a robust policy discussion.

Socially, Rwanda has made admirable progress in reconciling citizens from different backgrounds who have to live together in their communities, despite the atrocities of the past. Hundreds of thousands of people have been punished for crimes committed, and on a day-to-day level, many people are moving on with their lives. At the same time, barely a generation has passed, a short timeframe to overcome the horror that has been experienced. And while the country has set aside ethnic identity in favor of national unity, recovery naturally takes time and there is an awful lot that remains to be done over the generations to come.

Media and civil society are absolutely critical to creating the space for dialog, both about the past and about the policy issues to lay a bedrock for sustainable peace, participatory government, and effective long-term governance. Since 2006, we have built strong partnerships with local government and independent radio outlets and focused on building alliances based on shared interests. But it is imperative that there are capable organizations to facilitate sensitive dialogs on air and in person in an open environment, so to strengthen the capacity of media and civil society to work with authorities, and work with authorities themselves to engage the population in a constructive and inclusive manner.

In view of these few observations—and I am happy to share more—I want to make four recommendations, in conclusion, for U.S. policy. First, sustaining U.S. diplomatic engagement in Rwanda and the region is vital. I think there is unanimity from everyone in the room on that point. Although there are many competing demands for attention in the Great Lakes region alone, and let alone across Africa, this region can't be forgotten and it deserves a high-level focus within the region, adequate staffing and resources, both within the regional bureaus as well as within Embassies and USAID missions across the region.

While it may seem remote to many Americans, the horrors of genocide, civil war, and humanitarian crises that have been unleashed, and are still being unleashed in many parts of central Africa, have cost far too many lives, but also cost far too many dollars in international assistance focused on short-term palliation of chronic crises, rather than putting the region and its people on a path to a greater recovery.

Second, there are some things that the U.S. Government and the Congress should learn from the experience of conflict and recovery in Rwanda. Many conflict countries and fragile contacts have been beset by seesawing international attention focused on immediate short-term recovery, but not sustaining a holistic engagement to economic recovery, political participation, or reconciliation that are needed to sustainably transition from fragility. That is something that needs administrative action, but also congressional action to authorize and to support holistic approaches to conflict and fragility in the Great Lakes Region and beyond.

We recognize and appreciate the leadership that the Congress has shown on women, peace, and security, and salute the bill that just passed earlier this week. We also recognize the Eli Wiesel Genocide and Atrocities Prevention Act, which has been introduced back in May and can really make good on the U.S. commitment to Never Again.

Third, regional economic integration is critical, given the context of population density across the region and the need for radical economic transformation and a shared economic transformation. It is very clear that regional cooperation, which at the moment is quite beset between Rwanda, Burundi, DRC, and beyond, requires better cooperation across borders, but also people-to-people reconciliation to stabilize the wider region.

Finally, it is absolutely critical that the U.S. Government continue its support and accompaniment of Rwanda in overcoming the legacy of genocide and in reconciling itself to the horrific events of the past. Even though Rwanda has made much progress in dealing with the aftermath of genocide and the series of massacres that have marked its history, the horrific past and the related trauma still affect other avenues to a lasting peace and stability in Rwanda and in the region. Atrocities of this history and their consequences should pave the way to a much more open society where conflicts and differences can be dealt with openly and through dialog. The U.S. Congress should focus its engagement in working with the Rwandan Government in supporting the Rwandan people to build a brighter future and to achieve this goal together.

Thank you.

[The prepared statement of Mr. Jobbins follows:]

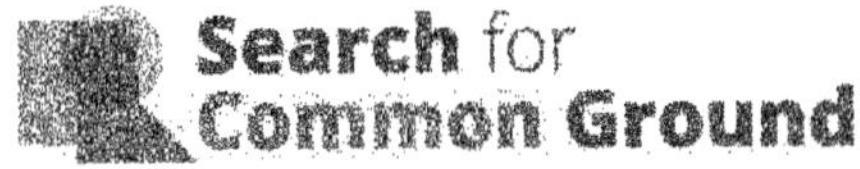

1601 Connecticut Avenue NW Suite 200,
Washington, DC 20009-1035 USA
T +1 202 265 4300 | F +1 202 232 6718
search@sfcg.org | www.sfcg.org

Rue Belliard 205, bte 13
B-1040 Brussels, Belgium
T +32 2 736 7262 | F +32 2 732 3033
brussels@sfcg.org | www.sfcg.org

House Foreign Affairs Committee

Sub-Committee on Africa, Global Health,
Global Human Rights, and International Organizations

Hearing on
Rwanda: Democracy Thwarted?

September 27th, 2017 – 3:00 p m
2200 Rayburn House Office Building

Statement of Mr. Mike Jobbins
Director of Global Affairs and Partnerships
Search for Common Ground

Chairman Smith, Ranking Member Bass, Members of the Committee, and distinguished guests, it is an honor to join you today. Thank you for convening this important hearing and for maintaining a focus on Africa's Great Lakes Region in general, and on Rwanda in particular.

I am the Director of Global Affairs with Search for Common Ground (Search), one of the largest organizations dedicated to transforming conflict in the Great Lakes region and around the world. Search was founded upon the philosophy that conflict is an inevitable part of human societies and is neither good nor bad. Problem-solving requires constructive debate and differences of opinion – between men and women, between groups, political ideologies, religions, or regions – and is the only way that any society can advance. But while constructive conflict can lead to more inclusive development and social outcomes, destructive conflict lead to violence, oppression and is the primary cause of extreme poverty and humanitarian need.

Search began its work in the Great Lakes in 1995, amidst one of the worst periods of destructive conflict in recent history. Search began working in Burundi amidst that country's civil war, looking at similar dynamics to those that fueled Rwanda's horrific genocide and supporting Burundians seeking to chart a different path, where media could bring people together and heal divides rather than ignite tensions and spark violence. Recognizing the shared challenges and important regional factors driving conflict throughout the Great Lakes, Search expanded its work to the Democratic Republic of Congo in 2001 and Rwanda in 2006 with the aim of supporting inclusive decision-making and reconciliation efforts.

Over the past decade, Search has worked closely with Rwandan government, media, civil society, and local communities to support reconciliation, address land disputes, and build the capacity of civil society and government institutions with a focus on youth. Search works with Rwandan partners including Government,[i] civil society, and media outlets across the country[ii] with support of grants from the U.S. government,[iii] European governments,[iv] UNICEF, as well as private philanthropists and foundations. While my testimony is informed by the time I have spent with Search, the opinions and perspectives are my own.

Twenty-three years following the genocide, Rwanda has seen impressive economic growth and a concerted effort from national and international actors to heal wounds and rebuild communities, and has been held up as a model of recovery and reconciliation. In the last decade, the country has faced three broad challenges: first, how to chart a path to economic growth overcoming the steep structural challenges that the country faced; second, how to establish post-conflict governance; and third how to ensure security nationally, with the regional implications in the troubled Great Lakes. I will focus my remarks on progress in these three sectors, with particular attention to women's participation, before offering a few recommendations for U.S. policy.

A Rapidly Transforming Economy and Agriculture Sector to Meet the Needs of a Growing Population

Rwanda has experienced dramatic economic growth. In the last 15 years, the economy has quintupled, from 1.3 to 8.3 billion dollars per year. The Rwandan economy is increasingly connected to the region and the wider world. Internet access has grown 250% since 2010, and more than a third of its GDP comes from global trade.[v] Much of Rwanda's economic growth has been driven by a transition away from subsistence economy and commodity exports towards greater value-added in the services and agricultural sector, facilitated by a regulatory environment that supports business and entrepreneurship and the Government's Vision 2020 plan for economic reforms.

This rapid growth has been even more striking considering the structural challenges that the country faced. Rwanda is landlocked, one of the most densely populated countries in the world and heavily dependent on subsistence agriculture. To illustrate the challenge: the UN estimates that Rwanda's population will nearly double by 2050.[vi] At the same time, the International Food Policy Research Institute forecasts that staple crop yields may drop due to changing soil productivity and climate change. This is a particular challenge for the young population. More than half of the population is under 20 years of age, and for the 80% who live in rural areas, access to land and agricultural productivity are critical to their future in terms of health, development, and the security of the country as a whole.[vii]

Addressing land scarcity. In this context of land scarcity, disputes over the allocation, access, and ownership of land remain the most common cause of conflict for ordinary Rwandans. The Government has tried to address this issue by adopting new policies and putting in place local conflict mediators known as *Abunzi*.[viii] While their mandate on mediation is broad, Search's research has found that approximately 80% of the cases they deal with are related to land. These local mediators are on the frontlines of challenging deep inequalities. For example, while women are legally entitled to inherit property, this right is not always recognized or respected in practice. Traditional norms and limited access to justice continue to obstruct women's ability to assert their rights, leaving them and their children economically and socially vulnerable. So, the Government is focused on incorporating women into the *Abunzi* structure, and it is starting to produce some early results in terms of supporting women's equal access to justice.

To support alternative dispute resolution (ADR) in this sector, Search partnered with the Ministry of Justice to provide training and coaching to 4,000 Abunzi community mediators, including female *Abunzi*;and with the National Women's Council to identify and train community resource people who could serve as advocates for marginalized groups, and particularly for women, as they tried to assert their rights to property and inheritance. Search has also been producing radio programming to ensure that rural residents had access to information on the latest land laws and policies and the opportunity to ask questions and raise concerns and conduct participatory theater performances that encouraged creative problem-solving so that families and communities could address land conflicts themselves, without needing the involvement of the over-burdened justice system. This partnership has thus far yielded promising results. For example, Search conducted a recent study in Gisagara District that and found an 85% satisfaction rate with female mediators, and that women's emerging leadership as *Abunzi* was opening entry points for their involvement in community decision-making fora, including within churches and other social settings.

Inclusive diversification. At the same time, given the demographic pressure, agriculture in its current form will not sustain Rwanda's growing population. There has been an important focus on developing alternative livelihoods and ensuring equal access to opportunities – particularly for rural youth and women – to benefit from the economic transformation. As in all societies undergoing rapid economic transformation, the poorest and least-educated struggle to take advantage of new opportunities in the services-oriented, globalized, and higher-technology economy. Impediments include a lack of information and access to opportunities, capital and education to seize opportunities, and a lack of exposure to role models and examples of entrepreneurship. Looking forward, emphasizing alternative livelihoods, and with an approach that recognizes the diverse needs and interests of the Rwandan population in this area, will be critical if Rwanda is going to meet its target of becoming a middle-income country

Search has worked with the Rwandan business community, radio, and television to help extend and popularize the opportunities created by the new economy. Search worked with Rwandan media producers to develop a weekly radio show highlighting vocational training and entrepreneurship opportunities and feature creative economic undertakings of young people, particularly aimed at rural audiences. Search also created *Zamuka,* a reality TV show akin to America's *Shark Tank,* which featured contestants learning the challenges, strategies, and paths to create a successful business. As one of the first TV reality shows produced in Rwanda by Rwandans, it succeeded in harnessing the diverse initiatives underway to support economic development, creating more information-sharing and cohesion among the various actors trying to support this sector.[ix]

Establishing Effective and Citizen Participation in Post-Conflict Governance

Rwanda is often celebrated as a champion of good governance on the continent. It ranks 44th out of 168 countries on the Transparency International's 2015 Corruption Perceptions Index[x] and 62 out of 189 in the World Bank's 2016 Doing Business report[xi], some of the best scores of any African country. At the social level, Rwanda has made admirable progress in reconciling citizens from different backgrounds who have to live together in their communities despite what role they played in the genocide. Hundreds of thousands of people have been punished for the crimes committed, and on a day to day level people are moving on with their lives. At the same time, not even 25 years is a very short timeframe to truly overcome the horror that the country experienced. While the country has set aside ethnic identity in favor of national unity as Rwandans, recovery naturally takes time and many still struggle with trauma.

Accountability, performance and participation. Rwanda has achieved these successes through a governance model that focuses on professional, results-oriented and technocratic governance with strong central leadership in policymaking and implementation. The strong coordinating role that the central government plays across society has helped stamp out corruption and driven a coherent policy agenda. Local officials are charged with balancing an emphasis on efficiency and a pressure to "deliver" with the impetus to create opportunities for citizen input and explain policy. The best local administrators create windows for citizens to tailor and shape policy implementation, but in other circumstances, Rwandan citizens struggle to find a window to feed into decision-making, and sometimes feel that policies are made despite them, rather than for their benefit.

Search has partnered with the Ministry of Local Government to foster inclusive and participatory governance to improve development outcomes with a particular focus on two-way communications and the relationship between local officials and citizens in the context of national policy reform. Jointly, Search has trained officials in different districts to support them on how to identify and manage rumors, build more active communications strategies, and work with local radio stations to provide better access to information and platforms for dialogue that can inform government about citizen concerns and feedback on existing policies. This partnership aims to reduce the need for top-down policy enforcement, towards better communication and alignment between officials and ordinary citizens around common long-term interests improving sustainability through ownership and participation.

Media and civil society have a key role to play in promoting sustainable peace and inclusive governance. Yet they face internal challenges that prevent them from fulfilling this role. Search has been working with the media sector since it began working in Rwanda in 2006, and it has built strong partnerships with both government and independent outlets that have common interests of mission and purpose at their core, rather than transactional exchanges. Civil society in general, and media in particular, remain a critical partner. Search will continue to leverage its Common Ground approach to strengthen the capacity of media and civil society to engage with the authorities and with the population in a constructive and inclusive manner. Search's experience has shown that investing in promoting diversity in the media sector can yield positive results. Search aims for inclusion in all of its media programs—at the national and regional level, seeking to include diverse perspectives and experiences to broaden listeners' understanding of a particular issue or concept.

Fostering women's participation. One of the other areas of dramatic progress has been in tackling structural gender issues. Rwanda has the highest percentage of women in National Legislature at 64%[xii], ranks 5th in the world for the equality of access to economic, health, and educational opportunities (the U.S. ranked 45th)[xiii], and has equal participation of girls and boys in the school system. This progress is remarkable, particularly against the backdrop of traditional patriarchal norms, and is attributable in many ways to the prioritization at the highest level. There is of course, still progress yet to be made, especially in rural areas where many Rwandan women face discrimination and violence within their household. Search has been working with the Ministry of Gender and Family as well as women leaders in civil society and in the media to help build the confidence and legitimacy to play a meaningful role in decision-making processes beyond the top level of politics.

High level representation has not yet been fully translated into protection and inclusion: over a third of women report that they have experienced physical violence in their lives, with 14% of women having experienced physical violence in the past year.[xiv] Through its work with *Abunzi* and local leaders, Search is working to address gender-based conflicts at the intra-household level, which are often related to land, inheritance, or decision-making. Search also worked with Rwandan media outlets and the *Association Rwandaise des Femmes des Medias* to improve the quality and availability of women's voices within the media sector, especially in the newsroom reporting (rather than human-interest, or "women's" issues), reached more than 2.5 million Rwandan listeners and found that more than three quarters of listeners across the region found that public access to good quality programs on gender and women's rights had increased.[xv]

Building Stability in the Wider Region

At the regional level, the Great Lakes and Central Africa remain profoundly unstable. Rwanda's relations with its neighbors continue to be challenging in a context of political crisis in the region, and especially in Burundi and the Democratic Republic of Congo (DRC). Diplomatic relations between Rwanda and Burundi have worsened since the Burundi crisis began in April 2015, driving a breakdown in the free movement of people and goods that have been critical to both countries' economies. With less trade, market prices of local goods are increasing, directly impacting ordinary citizens given the minimal cushion they have for price shocks. These tensions are particularly affecting small-scale petty traders, the majority of whom are women, who earn their survival selling agricultural products across the border.[xvi] Further, Rwanda is currently hosting more than 87,000 Burundians,[xvii] increasing the demographic pressure in the country. With crises and humanitarian calls to action in Somalia, South Sudan, and the DRC as well, there is little attention and limited resources to also attend to the Burundian situation and support its refugees. Past grievances in the region could also lead to further manipulation, population movements and deterioration of the economy, fueling cross-border violence that could lead to a regional conflict, especially as the DRC is heading towards a contentious electoral process.

To address misunderstandings and stereotypes in the wider region, Search developed a live regional call-in program. *Generation Grands Lacs* ran for nearly 10 years and reached millions from Matadi to Kigali.

highlighting young people's voices from Rwanda, Burundi and DRC as they sought to discuss and search for solutions to some of the region's long-running problems; evaluations found that the radio program reduced people's stereotypes about each other and contributed to better understanding and relationships between divided groups. Rwanda is an island of stability in a chronically fragile region, but long-term peace and economic growth for citizens throughout the wider Great Lakes Region relies on the entire region transitioning away from the legacy of violence and chronic fragility, and building a shared and inclusive future.

Key Recommendations

In view of these observations, I will conclude with four recommendations for U.S. policy.

First, sustain U.S. diplomatic engagement in Rwanda and the Great Lakes Region is vital. Although there are many competing interests and areas for the U.S. and the international community, the Great Lakes Region must not be forgotten and deserves high-level diplomatic attention. While the region may seem remote to many Americans, the horrors of genocide, civil war, and humanitarian crises that have been unleashed upon the citizens of Rwanda, DRC, Burundi, Uganda, South Sudan, and the Central African Republic in recent years continue to cost far too many lives and massive amounts of international assistance focused on saving lives rather than promoting growth. Rwanda is part of that context, and sustained diplomatic engagement is required both to sustain the U.S.-Rwanda partnership, and within the wider region. This is particularly true as President Kagame assumes the African Union Presidency in January, and as the U.S. continues to work with the region to support peace efforts in areas that are experiencing accentuated crises.

Second, learn lessons from Rwanda for other complex emergencies. Rwanda has made impressive gains in terms of security, development and reconciliation, but challenges still remain. Rwanda will continue to face dense population yet limited economic opportunities as a land-locked, resource-limited country; high expectations of economic growth and service delivery; and where the legacy of trauma still impedes collaborative problem-solving. Other fragile contexts in the region have been beset by see-sawing international attention and a lack of support for transitioning from emergency post-conflict assistance to reconciliation and economic recovery. At the same time, some of the legislation currently being considered by Congress, including the Elie Wiesel Genocide and Atrocities Prevention Act, seem to be promising windows to improve our own government's ability to respond to crises and prevent genocide.

Third, strengthen regional economic integration. Population density and environmental shocks pose existential threats to the entire Great Lakes Region. Sustaining the needed economic growth in Rwanda, and achieving growth in its neighbors, relies upon integration. Yet recent events have shown some of the weaknesses of regional structures. The Economic Community for the Great Lakes which brought together Rwanda, Burundi and DRC to address issues of common interests is not currently functioning. The ICGLR and the East African Community offer windows and frameworks for cooperation, but as recent conflicts within the region show, economic cooperation needs to be complemented by efforts that meet citizens' basic needs, support people-to-people reconciliation efforts, and lay the groundwork for dealing with the legacies of the past.

Finally, continue to support and accompany Rwanda in overcoming the legacy of the genocide and reconciling itself with the horrific events of the past. Even though Rwanda is making much progress in dealing with the aftermath of the genocide and a series of the massacres which marked its history, its horrific past and its related trauma still affect other avenues to lasting peace and stability in Rwanda and in the whole region. Atrocities of this history and their consequences in the aftermath should pave ways to a much more open society, where conflicts and differences are dealt with openly and through dialogue. The U.S. Congress should focus its engagement in working with the Rwandan Government and supporting the Rwandan people to build a bright future.

[i] Key Government partners include the Ministry of Justice, Ministry of Gender and Family Promotion, Ministry of Local Government, the National Commission for Unity and Reconciliation, the Rwanda Natural Resources Authority, and the Media High Council.

[ii] Media partners include the Rwanda Broadcast Authority, Radio Ishingiro, Radio Isangano, Radio Izuba, Radio Salus, Radio Isango Star, Contact FM, Radio and TV 10, and Radio Huguka.

[iii] This includes U.S. Agency for International Development's Office of Conflict Management and Mitigation, the U.S. Department of State's Bureau of Democracy, Human Rights and Labor, and the U.S. Institute of Peace

[iv] Including the Belgian, British, Dutch, Finish, and Swedish governments, as well as the European Union

[v] World Bank. *Rwanda Country Profile*. Washington, DC September 2017.

[vi] United Nations Department of Economic and Social Affairs. "*World Population Prospects 2017: Rwanda, Total Population, Probabilistic Projections*." DESA/Populations Division. 2017.

[vii] National Institute of Statistics of Rwanda. "Thematic Report: Population Size, Structure and Distribution" *Fourth Population and Housing Census of Rwanda*. Kigali, January 2014.

[viii] An excellent summary of this institution was published by the South African NGO Accord in : Mutisi, Martha. "*The Abunzi Mediation in Rwanda: Opportunities for Engaging with Traditional Institutions of Conflict Resolution*." *Accord Policy & Practice Briefs*. Mt. Edgecombe, South Africa, November 2011.

[ix] Nuwakora, Cliff Bernard. CASE International Consultants. *Final Report for the Progress Evaluation of SFCG's Entrepreneurship-Focused Initiatives Programme*. Kampala. September, 2014.

[x] Transparency International. *Corruption Perceptions Index 2015*. 2015.

[xi] World Bank Group. *Doing Business 2016: Measuring Regulatory Quality and Efficiency*. Washington DC 2016.

[xii] Inter-Parliamentary Union. "*Women in National Parliaments*." August 2017.

[xiii] World Economic Forum. "*Rankings: Global Gender Gap Index 2016*." 2016.

[xiv] The Rwanda Demographic and Health Survey. "*Rwanda: 2014-15 Demographic and Health Survey Key Findings*." Kigali 2015.

[xv] Chirhalwirwa, Pascal and Mary Myers. "*Media a Voice for All: Final Evaluation Report*." Search for Common Ground and iMedia. Washington, DC October 2014

[xvi] Kalisa, Narcisse and Gabrielle Solanet. "*Improving the Cross Border Trade Environment through Improved Research and Advocacy on Cross Border Trade Issues*." Search for Common Ground. Kigali February 2017.

[xvii] Representing over 21% of the total of Burundian refugees in the region; UNHCR figures, as of September 18, 2017. "*Refugees from Burundi related to the current situation – breakdown per country*." United Nations High Commissioner for Refugees. 2017.

Mr. SMITH. Thank you very much.
Mr. Akwei?

STATEMENT OF MR. ADOTEI AKWEI, MANAGING DIRECTOR, GOVERNMENT RELATIONS, AMNESTY INTERNATIONAL UNITED STATES

Mr. AKWEI. Thank you. I would like to thank you both for this opportunity to speak before your committee and, also, to acknowledge and thank your consistent engagement and leadership on issues related to Africa, human rights, and U.S.-Africa policy, which has been, and continues to be, essential and greatly appreciated.

Amnesty International is a global human rights movement established in 1961 with 7 million members and supporters. We have a presence in 70 countries and have offices in Dakar, Nairobi, Johannesburg, and Abuja. We have been working to improve the respect and protection of human rights in Rwanda since the early 1970s.

Amnesty does not take a position on the type of political system a country may have. It is our belief that fundamental human rights must be guaranteed and upheld by all political systems. We do consider the rights associated with elections such as freedom of expression, association, assembly, among others, to be critical not only to the election itself, but also to the overall health of open political space. The way governments engage with critics and voices of dissent, how they interact with civil society and treat human rights defenders are critical indicators that go beyond a single election.

With your permission, I would like to ask that our written testimony be submitted to the record.

Mr. SMITH. Without objection, so ordered.

Mr. AKWEI. The August 4th elections granted incumbent Paul Kagame his third term in office. This followed the referendum in 2015 which changed the constitution, allowing President Kagame to stand again in 2017 and for two further terms, should he desire to do so. In 2010, President Kagame won 93 percent of the vote; in 2017, he won 99 percent.

During the 23 years the Rwandan Patriotic Front has ruled the country there has been an unwavering and often brutal campaign against government critics and human rights defenders. This campaign has included a tax on political opposition members, including arrest, detention, disappearances and killings; restrictions on the media and the activities of civil society organizations, and the creation of a climate of fear. These concerns have been echoed by other human rights groups and the United States Department of State, which noted in its 2016 report: Government harassment, arrests, and abuse of political opponents, human rights advocates, individuals perceived to be a threat to government control and social order, restrictions on the media and the civil liberties. The attacks and the campaign have included, as mentioned above, attacks on the political opposition and, of course, the restrictions on the media and civil society.

In 2010, Amnesty reported that the authorities tightly controlled political space in advance of the 2010 elections. Freedom of expression was unduly restricted by broad laws on genocide ideology.

Human rights defenders continued to exercise self-censorship to avoid confrontation with the authorities, and conventional courts still fell short of fair trial standards.

In 2011, we reported that authorities restricted freedom of expression and association. Media outlets that criticized the government were closed down, editors fled, human rights defenders faced intimidation, investigations into killings were inadequate.

In 2012, Amnesty reported that the Rwandan Government increasingly prosecuted individuals for criticizing government policies and that there was a rise in unlawful detentions. Violations included restrictions that were imposed on freedom of expression arrests, unfair convictions of opposition politicians and of journalists.

In 2013, Amnesty reported that the government still continued to stifle legitimate freedom of expression and associations; that the illegal detention and allegations of torture by Rwandan military intelligence were not investigated. This was the same year that the Rwandan Government was also found by the U.N. group of experts to have provided military support to the M23 armed group in the neighboring Democratic Republic of the Congo, which was linked to rape, extrajudicial execution, and the use of child soldiers.

The government's crackdown and restrictions on expression, assembly, association, repression of journalists, human rights defenders, and member of the opposition parties who openly criticized the ruling government, use of unfair trials, and unlawful detentions were raised in our reports of 2014, 2015, and 2016. In 2017, we reported on the severe restrictions that we thought were going to color and shape the run-up to the elections. This was the result of over many years of the same types of actions.

It is time for the international community to press the Rwandan Government to change. Some have argued that Rwanda is still emerging from the 1994 genocide. Others have argued that, because Rwanda is doing well economically, the current administration should be given more latitude. These arguments must be rejected as they will subvert the common obligation to stand for rights accepted to be universal and that countries have committed themselves to, including Rwanda.

Amnesty International has called upon the Government of Rwanda to embark upon a longer-term reform process, to open up political space before the 2024 elections and, as you mentioned, before the 2018 parliamentary elections, and strengthen basic protections of rights beyond those.

The concerns I have outlined impact more than the next election, and addressing them will require more than a temporary easing of some laws, the release of a few people, or even the permission to register a political party or NGO. The assault on defenders and political space is quickening, and Rwanda is becoming a role model for the wrong things as opposed to the right things. It is not good for Africa. It is not good for the United States or for the global community, as history is littered with many examples of countries where political intolerance has led to political conflicts, and that has been extremely damaging. The global community failed Rwanda once before. It should not do so again.

Specifically, we would like to suggest that Congress and the Trump administration call on President Kagame and the Govern-

ment of Rwanda to prevent and ease restrictions on or the harassment of members of the political opposition, their supporters, on
journalists, and human rights defenders, and establish an independent judicial investigative mechanism into serious violations of
freedom of expression, assembly, and association. We have named
a number of specific individuals who have disappeared that should
be investigated.

Congress and the administration should also urge the Rwanda
Government to decriminalize defamation offenses and the review of
the Rwanda penal code. We would also urge the United States to
call on the Rwandan Government to reform the law on public assemblies and to remove the requirement for prior authorization for
public assemblies and, instead, a regime of prior notification.

We would also urge Congress to maintain and increase funding
for programs focused on building respect for human rights, the rule
of law, and independence of the judiciary. I would like to echo my
colleague from Search who raised the issue of building the capacity
of civil society and the media. These are critical institutions and
have to play their role in establishing, along with the Rwandan
Government, good governance, human rights, and respect for the
rule of law.

I will stop there. Thank you.

[The prepared statement of Mr. Akwei follows:]

The State of Human Rights in Rwanda
Statement by Amnesty International USA
before the House Subcommittee on Africa, Global Health, Global Human Rights and
International Organizations
Prepared by Adotei Akwei[1]

September 29, 2017

Chairman Smith, Ranking Member Bass and other members of the Subcommittee, on behalf of Amnesty International USA I would like to thank you for the opportunity to testify before this Committee. Your consistent engagement and leadership on issues related to Africa, human rights and US Africa policy has been and continues to be essential to making sure that issues and developments in the continent receive the attention they deserve, and in 2017 this function has become even more critical.

Amnesty International is a global human rights movement established in 1961 with 7 million members, offices in Dakar, Nairobi, Johannesburg, Abuja and a presence in 70 countries. We have been working to improve the respect and protection of human rights in Rwanda since the early 1970s.

Amnesty International does not take a position on the type of political system a country may have. It is our belief that fundamental human rights must be guaranteed and upheld by all political systems. We do consider the rights associated with elections such as freedom of expression, association, assembly among others, to be critical - not only to the election itself but also to the overall health of open political space. The way governments engage with critics and voices of dissent, how they interact with civil society and treat human rights defenders are critical indicators that go beyond a single election. With your permission, I would like to share our analysis and recommendations regarding the state of human rights in Rwanda for the record and look forward to discussing ways in which the United States and the international community can help Rwanda change course and avoid the further erosion of rights that has become a defining characteristic of the RPF administration.

---

[1] * With the help of Dr. Ken Harrow, Alana Smith, Essowe Telou, Rachel Nicholson and Christian Rumu

Background

The August 4 elections granted incumbent President Paul Kagame his third term in office. This followed a referendum in 2015 which changed the constitution, allowing President Kagame to stand again in 2017 and for two further terms should he so wish. During the 23 years that the Rwandan Patriotic Front has ruled the country there has been an unwavering, often brutal campaign against government critics and human rights defenders.
This campaign has included attacks on political opposition members including arrest, detention, disappearances and killings, restrictions on the media and the activities of civil society organizations and the creation of a climate of fear. These concerns have been echoed by other human rights organizations and the US Department of State which noted in its 2016 report that

The most important human rights problems were government harassment, arrest, and abuse of political opponents, human rights advocates, and individuals perceived to pose a threat to government control and social order; security forces' disregard for the rule of law; and restrictions on media freedom and civil liberties. Due to restrictions on the registration and operation of opposition parties, citizens did not have the ability to change their government through free and fair elections.

Other major human rights problems included arbitrary or unlawful killings; torture and harsh conditions in prisons and detention centers; arbitrary arrest; prolonged pretrial detention; government infringement on citizens' privacy rights and on freedoms of speech, assembly, and association; government restrictions on and harassment of some local and international nongovernmental organizations (NGOs), particularly organizations that monitored and reported on human rights and media freedoms; some reports of trafficking in persons; and government restrictions on labor rights; and child labor.

The government in many cases took steps to prosecute or punish officials who committed abuses, including within the security services, but impunity involving civilian officials and the SSF was a problem.[2]

Sadly, assessments of the government's performance regarding respecting human rights in lead up to the 2017 elections have not improved. Key human rights violations included

Attacks on Political Opposition

The government has actively cracked down on political opposition groups over many years.

On September 23, Diana Rwigara, along with her mother and sister, was arrested by Rwandan police accused of offenses against state security and forgery. Rwigara had tried to run against Kagame in the August 2017 elections before being disqualified. Shortly after she declared her intention to stand she was subjected to a smear campaign on social media.

---

[2] Rwanda, Country Reports on Human Rights Practices for 2016, Bureau of Democracy, Human Rights and Labor, March 2017

Unregistered opposition political party **FDU-Inkingi** has faced numerous restrictions since its president, Victoire Ingabire's, return to Rwanda in 2010 to attempt to stand in the 2010 presidential election. On the day of her return, she made a speech in which she discussed the lack of recognition of Hutus that had been killed during the genocide. She was sentenced to 8 years of prison for: "conspiracy to harm the existing authority and the constitutional principles using terrorism, armed violence or any other type of violence" and "grossly minimizing the genocide." Amnesty International is not in a position to assess the validity or otherwise of the terrorism-related charges in this case. During the trial, the judges showed open hostility toward her and constantly interrupted her despite the fact that the evidence used to convict her was linked to the legitimate expression of her ideas as guaranteed under the African Charter for Human and Peoples' Rights and the International Covenant on Civil and Political Rights. When she appealed her conviction to the Supreme Court on the basis of unfair trial, the Court said her claims were unfounded and lengthened her imprisonment to 15 years for spreading lies in order to incite the population to revolt against the current government.

In March 2016, another member of the **FDU-Inkingi** party, Illuminée Iragena, went missing, and another, Leonille Gasengayire was arrested for inciting insurrection, but was later acquitted. Both members were known to have visited Victoire Ingabire in prison. In September 2017, the party's vice-president Boniface Twagirimana, along with Leonille Gasengayire and several other members were arrested, accused of links to armed groups operating in a neighboring country.

Other opposition party figures such as members of **PS-Imberakuri** have previously been arrested and found guilty of "divisionism" for criticizing government policies. This follows the murder of the vice-president of the Green Party in 2010 and disappearances of various members.

<u>Restrictions on Independent Media and Civil Society</u>
The Rwandan government continues to suppress the independence and freedom of the media. Numerous journalists have been imprisoned, harassed and even killed, while many more have fled into exile over the years.

In 2016, at least three journalists were briefly detained after investigating sensitive issues, such as corruption or possible suspicious deaths on the part of the Rwandan government. The government also impedes the work of NGOs in the country through excessive registration procedures.

The BBC Kinyarwanda services were indefinitely suspended by the Rwanda Utilities Regulatory Authority (RURA) on 29 May 2015 after the broadcast of the documentary Rwanda's Untold Story, on the grounds that it violated Rwandan laws on genocide denial, revisionism, inciting hatred and divisionism.

The editor of *Umurabyo*, an independent Kinyarwanda-language newspaper, and her colleague were convicted in February 2011 on the grounds of articles they had written criticizing government policies and making corruption allegations against senior government officials, including President Kagame. While both were eventually released their incarceration is a chilling example of what journalists and human rights defenders in Rwanda risk for doing their jobs.

These actions mirror previous media crackdowns. The government suspended the newspaper *Umuvugizi* and another private Kinyarwanda- language newspaper *Umuseso* from April to October 2010, the same period as the 2010 elections. The Rwanda Media High Council then called for their indefinite closure claiming that some of their articles threatened national security.

Conclusions
Member of the Subcommittee, in 2010 President Kagame won 93% of the vote. In 2017 he won 99%. The concerns listed above are just some examples of the patterns of repression over the 23-year rule of the RPF.

In 2010, Amnesty reported that authorities tightly controlled political space in advance of the 2010 presidential elections, freedom of expression was unduly restricted by broad laws on genocide ideology, human rights defenders continued to exercise self-censorship to avoid confrontations with the authorities, and conventional courts still fell short of fair trial standards.

In 2011, we reported that the authorities restricted freedom of expression and association before presidential elections in August that year. Media outlets that criticized the government were closed down and editors fled Rwanda. Human rights defenders faced intimidation. Investigations into killings were inadequate. In 2012 Amnesty reported that the Rwandan government increasingly prosecuted individuals for criticizing government policies and that there was a rise in unlawful detentions. Violations included restrictions that were imposed on freedom of expression and the arrests and unfair convictions of opposition politicians and journalists. In 2013, Amnesty reported that the government continued to stifle legitimate freedom of expression and association and that the illegal detention and allegations of torture by Rwandan military intelligence were not investigated. That year the Rwandan government was also found by the UN Group of Experts to have provided military support to the M23 armed group in the neighboring Democratic Republic of the Congo (DRC) which was linked to rape, extrajudicial execution and the use of child soldiers. The government's crackdown and restriction on freedom of expression, assembly and association, repression of journalists, human rights defenders, and members of opposition parties who openly criticized the ruling government, use of unfair trials and unlawful detentions were raised in our Annual Human Rights Reports for 2014 2015 and 2016.

In 2017, we again reported on the severe restrictions human rights defenders, media and opposition politicians on their rights to freedom of expression, association and peaceful assembly in the run-up to elections this year and over many years.

The international community including the Clinton, Bush and Obama administrations have been at best half-hearted in confronting President Kagame and pressing the Rwandan government to reform its policies regarding human rights and political space. The Obama administration did press the Rwandan government and military to end their support of M23 but US leadership on human rights reform inside Rwanda has been at best tepid.

Some have argued that Rwanda is still emerging from the 1994 genocide. Others have argued that because Rwanda is doing well economically the current administration should be given more latitude. This argument must be rejected as it subverts our common obligation to protect and stand for rights that that have been adopted as universal.

Amnesty International has called on the Government of Rwanda to embark upon a longer-term reform process to open up political space before the 2024 elections. We expect the US government to support this call.

<u>Policy Recommendations</u>

Mr. Chairman, members of the subcommittee, the United States Government and the international community must speak up in defense of human rights defenders, journalists and civil society in Rwanda. Specifically, the United States should

1. Call on President Kagame and the government of Rwanda to prevent restrictions on, or harassment of, opposition candidates, their supporters, journalists and human rights defenders and establish an independent judicial investigative mechanism into serious violations of freedom of expression, assembly and association in past and present, including the murders of Andre Kagwa Rwisereka, Jean Leonard Rugambage and Jean Damascene Habarugira, as well as the disappearances of Illuminée Iragena and Jean Damascène Munyeshyaka;

2. Urge the Rwandan government to decriminalize defamation offences in the review of the Rwandan penal code;

   Call upon the Rwandan government to reform the Law on Public Assemblies to remove the requirement for prior authorization for public assemblies and instead adopt a regime of prior notification.

   Increase US funding for programs focused on building respect for human rights, the rule of law and independence of the judiciary.

Mr. SMITH. Thank you, Mr. Akwei. And thank you, all of you, for your tremendous input today. I do have a few questions I would like to ask.

One, I am concerned—and I have deep respect for Ambassador Yamamoto—that we seem to be overvaluing, the State Department, the U.S. Government, some facts like the participation of the Democratic Green Party, which got approximately 1 percent of the vote. Others who wanted to participate were precluded that opportunity, and then, as he said, the holding to account of the harassment of opposition candidates that was reported in the Rwandan media. Whether or not that is true, I still don't know. Was it a report, a false report, a sensational report that, oh, we are holding officials to account? That is not clear.

But, even in his own testimony, he goes on to say, as I quoted earlier, "Since the election, Rwandan authorities have targeted several political opposition figures for questioning and arrest." And then, he goes on and, accurately, quotes from the Country Reports on Human Rights Practices, pointing out arbitrary or unlawful killings by security forces, disregard for the rule of law, restrictions on civil society organizations, government interference with the press, which Mr. Akwei again and others have already made in their testimonies in terms of the crackdown on journalists. It is hard to call that some progress, frankly, when it seems to be going in the precisely opposite direction, where the percentage of the vote claimed by the President goes even higher than the previous one, and he is in for life based on the constitutional changes.

Your thoughts on that? Because I think we sometimes turn the page far too quickly, if it should be turned at all, and we are willing to look at one little seemingly bright, shiny object that we can, then, cling to, and it is a surface appeal argument. It has surface appeal that the Green Party participated, but what about all the others? It is a talking point that a lobbyist might want to push forward to a less-than-critical set of eyes and ears. So, I am concerned about that. Your thoughts on that, overvaluing this what I think is regression, not progress, by the Kagame regime?

Secondly, as you pointed out, Mr. Himbara—and I should have asked the Ambassador; I will by way of a written question—when you pointed out and brought further attention to Article 114, which gives immunity, which often means impunity. Because if you are not going to be held accountable ever for anything you do in office, including rape, having your soldiers rape and kill and extrajudicial killings, and the like, you are above the law completely for life. That needs to be much more further emphasized in our bilateral relations and, hopefully, in a multilateral way with Rwandans. If any of you would like to comment on that?

And I thought your point, Mr. Akwei—and I quoted it earlier, but it bears repeating—when you say, and you have so brilliantly, reported on severe restrictions on human rights defenders and the media, and the like, and you have done it painstakingly. You also point out that the international community, including the Clinton, George W. Bush, Barack Obama administrations, has been, at best, halfhearted in confronting President Kagame and pressing the Rwandan Government to reform its policy regarding human rights and political space. Those kinds of omissions on the part of bipartisan administrations is unconscionable because at the end of the day people get killed, women get raped and abused, people go to prison, journalists get harassed, and the people don't get the truth because it has a chilling effect on what they write.

So, if you could speak to that as well? Because now we have a new administration. It doesn't have all of its people in place yet. But we need to say clearly and unmistakably to the new White House: Don't repeat the bipartisan error of the past, because we will get the same outcome. We will get more impunity. So, whoever would like to go first? Yes?

Mr. HIMBARA. Mr. Chairman, very often we talk about a smoking gun. I think Article 114 is a smoking gun. Article 14, as you said, it is an opportunity. I wrote, in preparation for this hearing, I wrote—or I read as many constitutions as I could find anywhere, including even the constitution of the Democratic Republic of North Korea. I could not find a constitution that gives a green light to a head of state, not only to commit crimes while in office, but also after he has left office. So, I would assume that he is probably thinking that, after he leaves office, he will probably put in a puppet that would refuse to enforce international laws and say, "Look, you can't touch him here. He's here."

Because, as I said, there are cases here already in the U.S. And in the U.S., this is a country where even a sitting President can face law. So, really, the United States or even the United Kingdom, this is a country that—Rwanda is a member of the Commonwealth. How does the Commonwealth allow a country that gives a green light to criminality on the part of the head of state and get out of it?

So, here I would say that we should begin right there. We can plan for the removal, because either you want to be President and lead and build the economy and do these wonderful things, empower women—that is great. But, if you make a mistake, you cannot be above the law.

Thank you.

Major HIGIRO. Yes, thank you, Mr. Chairman.

Normally, I like to go into the details of, if what Mr. Jobbins just said, if what the State Department just said is true, whether it is government building institutions in Rwanda—so, what is the problem? Why is it that things are not working?

I asked him before he started that, if Rwanda can really develop so quick like they are saying—it is a landlocked country, we have neighbors—how do they do it? How do it that Burundi can't copy that, or Tanzania, or Uganda, or the DRC? What is the magic? And if there is no issue, why are we here?

So, I like bringing to this committee exactly what I am worried about. One, prisons criminalize Rwandans. And we all know when you push people to the wall what happens. How did we get to 1994? What really happened to get to 1994? It is this: We talk about issues and people choose which side they want to be on. They choose which truth they want to bring up. Personally, I can talk about the genocide because I was there. Sometimes Rwandans talk about the genocide; people have different views. But, when it comes to me as a soldier who tried to rescue people during genocide, I fought for 3 months before we took over. I know exactly what happened. I know how the Tutsis were being killed. I know of the crimes.

Then, we have what happened from 1994 to date. Again, I saw it until 2010, when I was decommissioned. I was serving the United Nations. I was a peacekeeper. I had two tours in Darfur, one as a commander of soldiers, another one as a staff officer heading the sector's information.

I know, too, that. I know how they work. I know the discipline of the Rwandan soldiers. I know where it comes from. And what I have been striving to give you and the State Department, and other elements of the government, is the truth. What people have to do with it is not up to me. But Kagame knows all this. He knows we are going to come here and make good speeches, talk about the corruption, and, you know, he will say corruption is everywhere in the world.

And most of the people who still go to Rwanda—it doesn't matter where you are working; it doesn't matter where you come from; it doesn't matter if you are Rwandan—in most cases, they will never criticize Rwanda. Do you know why? Because that is their end.

The previous region representative of the Great Lakes region, he failed to do his job. You either say what he is telling you or don't come back. And it doesn't matter which level they are on.

Now criminalizing Rwandans is in two ways. The Hutus, if you follow deeply, most of them are reluctant to talk about the current situation. Why? The moment you do that you become a genocider. Therefore, we have had cases for the Hutus, and some of them have been deported from the United States, have tried to engage with the United States Government about these cases. We are not saying we are supporting those who participate in genocide, no. We are saying we need fair justice. Try them here, right? Because there is no justice in Rwanda. No, that is the problem.

So, the Hutus have to keep quiet because they are genociders— that is it; no defense at all—everybody, even those who are born today. Kagame himself said, even if they are children, they have to be responsible for their parents' crimes. So, up to when are Hutus going to be free? We don't know as long as he is still living.

Now the second criminalization of Rwandans is the Tutsis. Today the opposition political parties in the diaspora, some of them have sympathizers inside the country, have raised the paranoia in the country to the government. So, even these recent arrests—for example, Diane Rwigara, I am very sure soon you will hear that she is part of those political parties.

We have a group of five political parties who form the coalition, and it is increasingly becoming stronger and, you know, they are gaining voice. I have spoken this or discussed this with the State Department because we always say, what is the alternative? Should we just say Kagame is bad and that is it? No. Rwandans have alternatives. They have seen that there is no Hutu government which is going to work; there is no Tutsi government which is going to work. That country was made for them both.

The reconciliation he talked about is a fake reconciliation. There is no way you can say that there is reconciliation in Rwanda. By picking a Hutu to become a prime minister every single time or some of them—he changed them in the middle of the term—does not mean reconciliation.

When Kagame has rallies in the western region where it is predominantly Hutu, when the Hutus show, it is a military operation. They start beating them up and driving them to the scene around midnight when Kagame is going to appear the next day around 3:00. Yes, that is what happens.

So, everything we see is a shawl. What they do, what Rwandans are concerned about, the Rwandan Government is concerned with two issues. When you get $400 million and you construct a trade center, a convention center, $400 million, what you are doing is protecting, showing the image of the country, right? Because $400 million can do a lot to the population, build schoolhouses, water, everything that they are lacking in the interior. So, the image of the country, that is what they show everybody who goes to Rwanda.

Two, the image of the President, it is only him who can do it, no one else. That is what they fight for. If you don't do it, that is it. Now, today it is not about the Hutus and Tutsis; it is everybody.

We have concerns with what is happening to families of these people who have already been killed, as has been mentioned. We have issues in the military. Four colonels were recently arrested and taken to unknown locations. It is in my submitted report. Many generals and colonels are out of a job.

And that is why I say that where we are today in Rwanda is where we were just before 1994. Suppose anything happened in Rwanda. Suppose Kagame got sick and died. What happens with all this tension?

Thank you, Mr. Chairman.

Mr. JOBBINS. Thanks for the question.

Just to focus on two things, I think one is, as we look at political discourse and the political life in Rwanda today, the way that we engage on these questions is fundamentally conflict and reconciliation. There is no such thing as a success in conflict resolution or reconciliation, neither here in America nor Europe nor anywhere. It is an ongoing process. Every political environment needs continual support to engage and develop a discourse that is healthy to participatory decision-making and to engagement. And Rwanda is no different from those.

I think, particularly as we look at the political life of ordinary Rwandans, to view as sort of a dichotomous absolutely success or absolutely failure misses some of the nuance that characterizes every society where we live and work.

Mr. SMITH. If you don't mind yielding briefly, my thought was that we give undue value, excessive applause to extraordinarily minor steps, while the steps backwards are very profound.

Mr. JOBBINS. Thanks. No, I absolutely——

Mr. SMITH. It is almost a straw man to think that any of us think we are perfect—there is no perfection. We strive to it, but when things are going in the wrong direction—that was the essence of the question.

Mr. JOBBINS. So, thanks. I really appreciate that.

What I wanted to sort of just underscore is, one of the things that is at least most vexing to us is, as we look at land, which is a life-and-death issue to ordinary Rwandans, the degree to which citizens understand necessarily the policies that impact them and have an opportunity to input into them is a continual process and quite uneven in terms of the way in which local governments, the way in which media, and others engage with citizens and lay that groundwork in bedrock for an informed policy debate.

And so, beyond sort of the policy and the political debates around elections, one of the things that we look for, and particularly in the U.S. focus on democracy in governance and the partnership with Rwanda in the context of dwindling resources, as Congresswoman Bass highlighted, is ensuring that there is adequate attention on building civil society capacity, supporting media, to cultivate and to build a context of constructive political discourse, both around development but also around the decisions that government takes. That is something that is in line with the vision that has been laid out by the government, but one where we see a need for continued improvement.

I think there is almost no place on earth, I might say, where the media environment has played a more negative role in the genocide. It was certainly profound thinking for our own organization how we engage in the role that media plays in societies. And almost no place where the social discourse has been as inflamed, and deliberately inflamed. And so, there is almost no place on earth where more attention needs to be paid to carving out and rebuilding a constructive media space, a constructive civil society, and free expression space; for citizens to really own and contribute to their own development in partnership with their government, but also in partnership with civil society and with other actors.

Mr. AKWEI. Thank you very much for the questions. I think I will just try to focus on the record of the previous administrations, which I know you, in particular, and Congresswoman Bass have fought very hard to try to correct.

A very good colleague and Africa expert once told me that good friends don't let their friends do bad things to themselves. And I think this is what happened, that there was, as one of the previous panelists mentioned, there was an overcompensation after 1994. There were regional tensions that were genuine and credible, and the Rwandan Patriotic Fund had the capacity and the ability to basically be a force for stability. But that was also accompanied by what Representative Bass said were genuine, incredibly impressive numbers in terms of economic, social, and cultural rights progress. No one is disputing that.

The challenge, I think, was that it became an "either/or." In other words, you are either in support of what was seen as an economic superstar, and any criticism of that was seen as a criticism of everything, which is extremely unfortunate because, what government and what country cannot have flaws as well as successes? Africa is no different.

I think this has also become part, unfortunately, of the mindset of the government, that critiques or questions about certain policies tend to be equated with critiques about the government itself, whether legitimate or not. And that has descended into a reticence going back to the Clinton administration and the Bush administrations and the Obama administration, where there was a reluctance, or it was almost a struggle to get them to challenge and to actually take the Department of State reports, which consistently documented the shortcomings, and do something about it.

And I think your point is right, we may not have the luxury to discuss the past, but we have the present and the future. The Trump administration has to adopt a different tact because, as our colleagues have said, the pressure is building. There are trends now where the political space is closing, and Rwanda is usually referred to as the epicenter. That, I think, is extremely alarming because, as one of my colleagues just said, wasn't that similar to where we were just before 1994, when there was no space and no ability to engage in dialog? Not simplifying things, but that is not where we want to go back to.

Ms. BASS. Thank you, Mr. Chair.

I wanted to ask in terms of the government and from the perspective of the U.S. what type of external pressure and which messengers tend to have the most positive impact. I would ask that of Mr. Jobbins.

Mr. JOBBINS. Thanks a lot.

I think in terms of what we see as being constructive, the challenge is there is a risk in overestimating the role that external players and external pressure can play on shifting a political environment or in assuming that all that is needed is political will, rather than also forging a political way.

And so, even though I think some of my colleagues have spoken about the concerns about public discourse, self-censorship, like Adotei highlighted, but that is also about encouraging positive models, supporting examples of how citizens have engaged in creating role models that can craft and foster constructive participation from citizens to their own development and to the ultimate sort of you contribute to political life.

Ms. BASS. So, let me ask you a little bit about that, because I believe your organization is engaged in some of that. And so, I wanted to know how you would assess the progress of reconciliation and peace building in Rwanda and how it might compare with other countries in the region.

Mr. JOBBINS. Sure, absolutely.

I think, as many of you know, Rwanda has taken a very different tact; for example, its colleagues or the neighbor to the south in Burundi. There has been a very strong consensus forged in Rwanda to move beyond an identification of the past with Hutus and Tutsis, craft a national identity that we are all Rwandans. That is something that characterizes Rwandan society today. It is something that I believe, from interactions with Rwandans myself and others, it seems to be something that is broadly accepted.

We have worked with NURC, the National Union and Reconciliation Council. And it is one that is obviously a different tact from how, for example, we deal with difference here in America. Here we talk explicitly about racial differences. We also talk about our own history in a way that is different, for example, from Brazil that has experienced similar differences. Every society deals and defines—whether it is class, religion, race, ethnicity, the divisions that make it up are phrased differently and understood differently as a legacy of history, as a legacy of culture, and as a deliberate choice about the vocabulary that people choose to use to describe themselves and to describe their neighbors.

The push toward reconciliation, and to move beyond that fram-ing, from all that we can see, appears to be in the surveys that we have done, is quite genuine and felt by ordinary Rwandans. The memory of the genocide, the desire to prevent that, again, animates political life, but that doesn't mean that there is not path depend-ency. That doesn't meant that where you are today is completely divorced from where your family was 25 years ago. And so, there is a degree of differences linked to the past that can only be really addressed with dialog.

Ms. BASS. I know that they are going to call votes in a minute, but I appreciate that.

Mr. Higiro, I think I heard you say that some of the opponents of Kagame have been deported from the U.S.? Did you say that?

Major HIGIRO. No, it was not the opponents. The Hutus who have cases linked to genocide crimes, yes, which have been fab-ricated.

Ms. BASS. Oh, I see.

Major HIGIRO. Yes.

Ms. BASS. They were deported from here?

Major HIGIRO. Yes.

Ms. BASS. Recently?

Major HIGIRO. It is about a few months.

Ms. BASS. Okay.

Major HIGIRO. The last case I know at least is a few months.

Ms. BASS. I don't think certainly anybody in this room feels that there is not a ton of problems that have to be dealt with in Rwan-da. As I stated in the beginning, I think our chairman laid it all out.

But I am concerned, though, that if you paint a country as com-pletely negative in this political environment that we are in, where they are calling for, the administration is calling for a 30 percent cut in the State Department, that you can have a situation where people just walk away, too. I don't think that that would be posi-tive on any account. People have to feel as though there is some hope. Otherwise, what is the point?

So, those are my only questions. I do have to say, though, that I thought it was rather unfortunate that you seem to be pretty dismissive of the women parliamentarians in Rwanda, who I meet with. They come here, as I meet with parliamentarians and women leaders from around the world. I don't doubt the fact that it might be a rubberstamp, but I don't think that the women view them-selves as irrelevant. I do think that women around the world do look at that number and think that it is pretty impressive.

I yield back my time.

Mr. SMITH. Thank you.

I will just ask one final thought, or question, I should say. Many have mentioned, including our Ambassador, the plight of Diane Rwigara. If I have this correct, she has pointed out that, she has criticized Kagame and his ruling Rwanda Patriot Front for acquir-ing a $500 million business empire, Crystal Ventures.

I introduced a bill just the other day, this week, on Azerbaijan's ongoing and egregious human rights abuses, particularly political prisoners. When I introduced the similar bill in the last Congress, and it was roundly criticized by the Baku government, I had met in Azerbaijan a journalist, Khadija, who had exposed Aliyev's corruption. She was a reporter for Radio Free Europe. We had a hearing when she was incarcerated, and the head of Radio Free Europe came to this room and testified. She was eventually freed. I don't know how free she remains. But journalists who take that kind of risk—she had gotten a 7½-year prison sentence—but no mention was made by the White House to protest it, although Radio Free Europe did, thank God.

I often find when you raise an issue that is country-specific, they somehow think you have some ill will toward that country. And certainly Azerbaijan did that. Vietnam does it routinely when I introduce the Vietnam Human Rights Act, which has passed three times in the U.S. House. It never got past the Senate. When I wrote the Belarus Democracy Act of 2004, which held Lukashenko's government to account and imposed visa denials and very significant economic sanctions against his businesses, he denounced it. And I was just in Belarus a few months ago. And we are getting the same kind of pushback from Rwanda, that somehow we are singling out. And I do it with China. I have done it with many countries around the world where I have had country-specific human rights bills, some of which have become law, like Belarus, and now, the most recent one this week was on Azerbaijan. Last time, like I said, it was roundly and derisively criticized by the Baku government. Kagame has got the same view. This has nothing whatsoever to do with anything but compassion and empathy and concern for the people of Rwanda—they deserve better.

So, my question is—we have talked about the human rights situation, the attacks on journalists, the attacks on individual people, the attacks on Mr. Higiro and the threats that he faced. My question is, do we know if Paul Kagame has amassed a fortune anywhere? We often find even Yasser Arafat—who was supposedly fighting tooth and nail on behalf of the Palestinian people—upon his death, we learned that he amassed a fortune that would have been well utilized for the people under Palestine Liberation Organization (PLO) control. And, yes, he was a rich man, and we find that all over the world.

So, do you have any information or could you, if necessary, get back to the committee, about Kagame's personal fortune? Does he have one? Yes?

Mr. HIMBARA. When the Panama Papers came out, I think it was last year, something extraordinary happened. He is the only President in Africa that I know of that featured his assistants. And I say it was extraordinary because elsewhere there was uproar about the Panama Papers. But, because of the situation in Uganda, no single paper would even dare discuss the Panama Papers. It took nothing.

Mr. SMITH. For the record, what was contained within the Panama Papers?

Mr. HIMBARA. Oh, what was concerned is that he had, they have offshore accounts that operate aircraft, private aircraft. Now we know that in Crystal Ventures, Crystal Ventures is Kagame, and

RPF don't deny that Crystal Ventures exists. Crystal Ventures has more employees than even the central government. This is open.

Crystal Ventures thrives on cronyism, basically, contracts from the government. Any opposition, any competition to Crystal Ventures, destroyed. So, what is going on there is that, even with clean records of corruption, see, what the report is about is petty corruption. But, when we talk about institutionalized corruption, then we are talking about something else.

The Crystal Ventures is open. Crystal Ventures has aircraft; this is known, $60 million apiece. And what do these two aircrafts do? They shuttle the President. So, the President basically rents his aircraft from—so, there is Kagame, the President, renting aircraft from Kagame, the chairman of Crystal Ventures.

What is extraordinary is that all this is in the open. Now the problem is no media in Rwanda would dare talk about this, but foreign media is doing this. I refer to The Economist. Two months ago, I think the title is—no, I forgot, but I will send you. I will refer it to the committee.

The case of Crystal Ventures, the case of, you know, like transferal of public resources from the government to Crystal Ventures, even these loans he spoke about them, $4 million, that has built the convention center. Government went into debt for that money, but, suddenly, the owners of these hotels are who? Crystal Ventures.

Major HIGIRO. Mr. Chairman, we have evidence of offshore accounts which we can always bring to your office.

Mr. SMITH. We will ask the State Department if they have any knowledge of any personal corruption for President Kagame and whether or not he has accumulated wealth that would not be commensurate with the job of a President.

Anybody else like to add? But I do have to run. We have only a few minutes left.

We deeply appreciate your testimony, your insights. It helps enlighten, especially with the new administration. So, thank you so very, very much.

The hearing is adjourned.

[Whereupon, at 5:03 p.m., the subcommittee was adjourned.]

APPENDIX

MATERIAL SUBMITTED FOR THE RECORD

SUBCOMMITTEE HEARING NOTICE
COMMITTEE ON FOREIGN AFFAIRS
U.S. HOUSE OF REPRESENTATIVES
WASHINGTON, DC 20515-6128

Subcommittee on Africa, Global Health, Global Human Rights, and International Organizations
Christopher H. Smith (R-NJ), Chairman

September 26, 2017

TO: MEMBERS OF THE COMMITTEE ON FOREIGN AFFAIRS

You are respectfully requested to attend an OPEN hearing of the Committee on Foreign Affairs, to be held by the Subcommittee Africa, Global Health, Global Human Rights, and International Organizations in Room 2200 of the Rayburn House Office Building (and available live on the Committee website at http://www.ForeignAffairs.house.gov):

DATE: Wednesday, September 27, 2017

TIME: 3:00pm

SUBJECT: Rwanda: Democracy Thwarted

WITNESSES: Panel I
The Honorable Donald Yamamoto
Acting Assistant Secretary
Bureau of African Affairs
U.S. Department of State

Panel II
Mr. David Himbara
Coordinator for Canada
Democracy in Rwanda Now

Major Robert Higiro, Rwanda Defense Force, Retired
Coordinator for the United States
Democracy in Rwanda Now

Mr. Mike Jobbins
Manager
Africa Programs
Search for Common Ground

Mr. Adotei Akwei
Managing Director
Government Relations
Amnesty International United States

By Direction of the Chairman

COMMITTEE ON FOREIGN AFFAIRS

MINUTES OF SUBCOMMITTEE ON _Africa, Global Health, Global Human Rights, and International Organizations_ HEARING

Day _Wednesday_ Date _9/27/17_ Room _2200_

Starting Time _3:00pm_ Ending Time _5:03pm_

Recesses |___| (___to___) (___to___) (___to___) (___to___) (___to___) (___to___)

Presiding Member(s)

Smith

Check all of the following that apply:

Open Session ☑
Executive (closed) Session ☐
Televised ☐

Electronically Recorded (taped) ☐
Stenographic Record ☑

TITLE OF HEARING:

Rwanda: Democracy Thwarted

SUBCOMMITTEE MEMBERS PRESENT:

Bass

NON-SUBCOMMITTEE MEMBERS PRESENT: _(Mark with an * if they are not members of full committee.)_

HEARING WITNESSES: Same as meeting notice attached? Yes ☑ No ☐
(If "no", please list below and include title, agency, department, or organization.)

STATEMENTS FOR THE RECORD: _(List any statements submitted for the record.)_

Each witness submitted written statement for the record

QFRs sent on 10/5/17

TIME SCHEDULED TO RECONVENE ________
or
TIME ADJOURNED ________

Subcommittee Staff Associate

Questions for the Record Submitted to
Acting Assistant Secretary Donald Yamamoto by
Representative Chris Smith (#1 to #4)
Subcommittee on Africa, Global Health, Global Human Rights, and International Organizations
September 27, 2017

Question 1:

Why has the State Department not taken a tougher line on human rights violations in Rwanda over the past decade? Does it involve concern over losing the Rwandan partnership in peacekeeping?

Answer 1:

The State Department has repeatedly expressed our concerns about human rights in Rwanda. In both public and private, we have called on the Government of Rwanda to respect human rights and fundamental freedoms – such as the rights to freedom of expression, peaceful assembly, and freedom of association – and to protect all persons from arbitrary arrest or detention. For example, we publicly expressed concern on August 5 over voting irregularities observed during the August 4 election, the integrity of the vote-counting process, and the lack of transparency in determining the eligibility of prospective candidates. We have also raised concerns regarding harassment of opposition leaders; security forces' disregard for the rule of law; and undue restrictions on NGOs, media freedom, and civil liberties. Our annual human rights and trafficking-in-persons reports for Rwanda candidly report our findings. We have also underscored these concerns within the context of the eligibility criteria for the African Growth and Opportunity Act. Rwanda is an important partner in peacekeeping cooperation, but this does not diminish our concern over human rights violations and abuses in Rwanda or our willingness to act upon those concerns.

Question 2:

During the 1990s, Paul Kagame was labelled one of Africa's "new leaders." To what extent has he lived up to the expectations that led to that designation?

Answer 2:

Under President Kagame, Rwanda has made remarkable gains in the fields of health, poverty reduction, access to education, and economic development. President Kagame's data-driven approach to development initiatives and the accountability he demands from his government have made Rwanda a model in leveraging development assistance into concrete results for its people. Rwanda has also reduced its dependence on foreign assistance by more than half in the last decade. At the same time, we are concerned by President Kagame's authoritarian leadership and the Government of Rwanda's intolerance for dissent, including restrictions on freedom of expression, press freedom, and the right of peaceful assembly. We are also concerned about the repression of opposition leaders, journalists, and human rights defenders. In January 2016, the State Department expressed public disappointment with President Kagame's decision to seek a third term, and we continue to press him on his plans for a democratic transition.

<u>Question 3:</u>

In his testimony, Mike Jobbins of Search for Common Ground recommends continued U.S. engagement with Rwanda in the East Africa region. How successful has our two countries' alliance been in addressing regional issues?

<u>Answer 3:</u>

Rwanda has been an important contributor to peace and security on the continent. Rwanda is the fifth-largest contributor of peacekeepers in the world. Rwandan troops have participated in UN peacekeeping operations in the Central African Republic, Sudan, and Mali. In South Sudan, Rwanda recently deployed additional peacekeeping troops as part of the UN's Regional Protection Force. Rwandan troops are disciplined and regionally respected. Rwanda is a priority partner in the Africa Peacekeeping Rapid Response Partnership (APRRP), and in the African Union (AU), it has been a leader in pressing for reforms so that the AU is better prepared to resolve regional conflicts. At the same time, we acknowledge that Rwanda has had a difficult relationship with its immediate neighbors in the past. These relations have improved over the past few years, as evidenced by the adoption of a three-country single visa for Rwanda, Uganda, and Kenya in 2014 and the reduction of trade and non-trade barriers under the aegis of the East Africa Community. We are committed to ensuring that these relations further develop to support the region's development, security, and stability.

Question 4:

The State Department long declined to accept the various UN reports on Rwandan involvement in smuggling of resources from the Democratic Republic of the Congo or support for militia inside that country. Is the view in the Department of Rwandan involvement on these issues any different today?

Answer 4:

The State Department has now and in the past, taken UN reports very seriously, including the various Group of Experts' reports on the Democratic Republic of the Congo. These and other credible reports of Rwandan support for the M23 – an armed rebel group that committed trafficking crimes through the forcible and fraudulent recruitment and use of children and men – led the United States to suspend military assistance to Rwanda and downgrade Rwanda to Tier 2 Watch List in the annual Trafficking in Persons Report in 2013. Pressure from the United States and the international community led Rwanda to cease its support to the M23 in 2013. In September 2014, President Obama certified that Rwandan assistance to the M23 had ceased, and U.S. military assistance to Rwanda resumed. We support international efforts to curb illegal smuggling of resources in the Great Lakes region, as this trafficking contributes to criminality, supports militias and rebel movements, and adds to insecurity throughout the region. We remain committed to the mandate of the Group of Experts, including their recent reporting on resource smuggling.

Questions for the Record Submitted to
Mr. David Himbara by
Representative Chris Smith
Subcommittee on Africa, Global Health, Global Human Rights, and International Organizations
September 27, 2017

Mr. David Himbara, Coordinator for Canada, Democracy in Rwanda Now

QUESTION: According to your testimony, both the United States and United Kingdom found serious fault with the August reelection of President Kagame. Why do you think more wasn't made of that view after the elections were declared to be tainted?

HIMBARA: The United States and the United Kingdom stated publicly that the August 2017 reelection of Kagame was flawed in two ways: 1) credible candidates were barred from elections; 2) vote tabulation was manipulated. However, the US and the UK have not done anything about the flawed elections in Rwanda. This has become routine. The two countries make a bit of noise and goes back to business as usual with Kagame. This is a replay of the 2010 elections. I think the two countries have invested in Kagame no matter what. This is unfortunate. Investing in a dictatorship does not pay in the long run.

QUESTION: People voted in a large percentages for President Kagame in the 2015 referendum and the 2017 elections. Do you feel the average Rwandan believes in the success of the Kagame government, or are they voting for the best known candidate available?

HIMBARA: Leading political opposition personalities are either in prison or in exile - and some have died mysteriously. Diane Shima Rwigara is the latest victim to be thrown in jail for challenging Kagame. Diane Shima Rwigara, her mother Adeline Rwigara, and her sister Anne Rwigara, face charges of plotting to overthrow the Kagame regime. This is the environment in which Kagame "wins" elections and referendum to change the constitution. He is the only so-called candidate imposed on the Rwandan people.

QUESTION: If the United States cuts off military aid to Rwanda, wouldn't that hamper Rwanda's involvement in peacekeeping missions? Don't you think that is why such an action has not been taken by the United States to this point?

HIMBARA: There are many African governments that receive military support from the United States. These include countries that do not commit atrocities on their own people or don't cause havoc in neighbouring like Rwanda does. It is not as if Africa has only one that can keep peace. There are options. Tanzania, Kenya, Nigeria, South Africa, Ghana, Malawi, Zambia, and Senegal are democratic nations that have capable armies to partner with in peacekeeping. It does not make any sense to promote an army in peacekeeping abroad while the same army makes war at home and in the neighbourhood.

Questions for the Record Submitted to
Mr. Robert Higiro by
Representative Chris Smith
Subcommittee on Africa, Global Health, Global Human Rights, and International Organizations
September 27, 2017

Mr. Robert Higiro, Coordinator for United States, Democracy in Rwanda Now

1. You cite in your testimony the disappearances of political opponents of President Kagame. Why has this not been given wider attention on the international stage?

(a). The international community was compromised for failing to stop genocide and Mr. Kagame uses it to attack anybody who calls him out. (b). The false narrative of a developmental state (Rwanda) has been hyped over the years (World Bank, IMF, and donor countries). They are shy to retract themselves (praises) having realized the lie. Others are dying for a 'success' story to justify aid. (c). Rwanda has been categorized as a United States ally and sometimes human rights issues are overlooked not to annoy allies. (d). Rwanda runs numerous well-funded PR firms who constantly challenge critics and keep helping on 'positive' propaganda. They dominate the social media and print overwhelming criticisms.

2. You have described Rwandan government destabilization of the Democratic Republic of the Congo and Burundi and the assassinations of Rwandan dissidents in other countries. Why have these governments or regional organizations, including the African Union, not done more to counter these actions by the Kagame government?

(a). A number of countries have deported Rwanda diplomats (Uganda, Kenya, Democratic Republic of Congo, Burundi, Sweden, Germany, France & South Africa). Four people were tried and sentenced to 8 years in South Africa. (b). The African Union is now dominated by dictators; some governments are doing the same in their own countries. There is no moral authority for most of them to call out the government of Rwanda.

3. You say that Rwanda is back in a climate that existed prior to the 1994 genocide. Can you describe what you mean by that allegation?

(a). Mr. Kagame's predecessor President Habyarimana was scoring 98% in elections and so is President Kagame. So, political space is closed for peaceful transfer of power. Rwandans may resort to violence as was the case in 1990.

(b). Amendment of constitution virtually making Mr. Paul Kagame president for life, just like how the previous president Juvénal Habyarimana's tenure was also uncertain and people supported war because peaceful means were not possible. (c). Militarization of the population and creation of auxiliary forces work like former president Habyarimana's militia and they may massacre people in case of challenge to the regime. (d). Imprisonment, killings and disappearances were common occurrences during the 1990s, but it is more prevalent now. The state of fear and terror is even more felt now than the people felt in the 1990s. (e). The question of refugees, which prompted the Rwandan Patriotic Front to take arms is the same condition that obtains now. Rwanda is churning out more refugees and this is recipe for potential violence.

Questions for the Record Submitted to
Mr. Mike Jobbins by
Representative Chris Smith
Subcommittee on Africa, Global Health, Global Human Rights, and International Organizations
September 27, 2017

Mr. Mike Jobbins, Manager, Africa Programs, Search for Common Ground

Question: The image many people have of Rwanda is of an authoritarian state that seeks to punish those considered dissidents. However, you describe a country in which reconciliation is a primary goal throughout the country. How can we square these two images of Rwanda?

Answer: Twenty-three years after the genocide, history is still a daily part of Rwandan public life and culture. The trauma of the genocide is still felt very deeply and while there has been great progress, it is a process that is by no means finished. Many Rwandans do believe there is a risk of resurgence. The 2010 Rwanda Reconciliation Barometer, compiled and released by the National Unity and Reconciliation Commission surveyed Rwandans on reconciliation and what progress they saw on some of the common-cited root causes:

> "The results show that an overwhelming majority of respondents (97.9%) do feel that the way in which history was conveyed from one generation to another has contributed to major divisions in society, and as a result 94.7% indicated that they felt that the current approach to its teaching is far more conducive to the promotion of reconciliation. A considerable majority (87.0%) also agreed that in the sixteen years following the genocide most of the major issues related to its causes and consequences have been frankly discussed and understood. A somewhat lower level of agreement (59.3%) was registered for the statement, which proposed that conflicts between members of the political elite has been effectively managed. Agreement levels for those that agreed with the suggestion that "many of Rwanda's conflicts can be blamed on ethnic manipulation" (69.7%), are also less emphatic than those for most of the other statements. A result, which may be of concern and should be taken note of, is the fact that 39.9% of respondents agreed that "although it is against the law, some Rwandans would try to commit genocide again, if conditions were favourable". This does raise questions about respondents' sense of human security and may need further probing."

Reconciliation in Rwanda – as in many places where we work – is a long-term process of healing social rifts, and requires investment by government, civil society, media and the wider citizenry to build relationships at every level: in the cells and districts, as well as within the national political space. The majority of Rwandans actively work towards reconciliation and are engaged in the effort of making sure that the past does not repeat itself. An open society is central to fostering reconciliation, where citizens can feel confident to discuss the legacies of the past and resolve future conflicts. This requires support from every level, including the National Unity and Reconciliation Commission, civil society organizations (CSOs) and non-governmental organizations (NGOs) like Search for Common Ground.

Question: Your organization works on alternative dispute resolution, as you stated, training the Abunzi community mediators. Along with the gacaca traditional courts process used for genocide trials, do you think Rwandan dispute reconciliation procedures can be translated to other countries?

Answer: Generally speaking, the dispute reconciliation processes carried out in Rwanda can be translated to other countries, and there are a lot of lessons to learn. Every society is unique, and relying on local traditional institutions – and what functionally works in daily life – is critical to supporting local dispute resolution. In Rwanda, the *abunzi* play this role. At the same time, most observers would recognize that any Alternative Dispute Resolution (ADR) institution, whether governmental, non-governmental, or traditional, would need ongoing training and support. We provide both direct support, as well as to their role within the wider system. In Rwanda we provide training and coaching directly to the *abunzi*, but also work with the Ministry of Justice to ensure that there is a coordination between the two. One of the key results that we have seen in Rwanda is the benefit that training has had on ensuring women's participation within the *abunzi* institution, and build skills and public confidence in women mediators. In Gisagara, for example, we saw that after training and support, 85% of the public felt confident in women mediators.

The role that traditional and informal institutions can play in resolving disputes and preventing conflicts from escalating is often neglected. We also work with the *judiyya* of Sudan and South Sudan, traditional leaders in the Democratic Republic of Congo, and the *bashingantahe* in Burundi to provide ADR services. Elsewhere, we've seen other kinds of informal structures step into these roles that are not "traditional" but still provide access to justice, including paralegal-type mediation organizations in Niger and Chad that focus on farmer-herder disputes and *Comités de Paix et de Médiation (CPMs)* in the Central African Republic which link community, traditional and religious leaders to resolve disputes. None of these institutions are perfect, like all other elements of society, they have been warped by war and struggle to involve youth, women, and minority populations. Yet, they are often able to deliver justice practically in areas outside of the courts and resolve thorny land and other local disputes.

Question: Rwanda portrays itself as a rapidly overcrowded country, and you cite UN estimates of a doubling of the population by 2050. How efficiently is Rwanda using all of its territory, especially rural areas, for development that can prevent overcrowding in cities and towns?

Answer: Rwanda does not have quite the same urban migration challenge as other African countries, in the sense that there is not the same overwhelming move towards the capital. However, it does face the challenge that most of the population (around 85%) relies on subsistence agriculture, which is not sustainable with a growing population. Land use management and planning is a central component of Vision 2020, which writes:

> "Land use management is a fundamental tool in development. As Rwanda is characterized by acute land shortage, a land use plan has been developed to ensure its optimal utilization in urban and rural development. Currently, Rwanda's scarce land resources still face a challenge of ineffective translation of the developed land use master plan into sector strategic plans and district development plans. In the coming years, Rwanda will ensure that every development plan is guided by the land use master plan. The recent land tenure regularization will increase security on ownership and improve productive land usage."

The government is experimenting with new solutions to address this problem, and Vision 2020 goes on to lay out a vision of moving towards grouped settlements (rather than scattered "homestead" style housing), in order to stimulate local industry and eventually support modernized farming. It lays out:

> "Rwanda will continue to pursue a harmonious policy of organized grouped settlements (umudugudization). Rural settlements organized into active development centres will be further equipped with basic infrastructure and services. While this system of settlement will continue to serve as an entry point into the development of non-agricultural income generating activities, land consolidation will be emphasized so as to create adequate space for modern and viable farming."

This is an ambitious vision and transformation of daily lives. Like I noted in my testimony, one of the critical challenges in rolling out this vision lies in how well local administrators can incorporate citizen input into the way that these policies are practically applied and shaped, while also cohering with the overall roll out. To that end, media, civil society, and other vectors of citizen input are critical within the wider policy rollout.

Questions for the Record Submitted to
Mr. Adotei Akwei by
Representative Chris Smith
Subcommittee on Africa, Global Health, Global Human Rights, and International Organizations
September 27, 2017

Mr. Adotei Akwei, Deputy Director, National Advocacy and Government Relations, Amnesty International USA

You describe an authoritarian government that has created a climate of fear. If a Rwandan citizen is not involved in politics or advocacy, would he or she still be aware of the climate of fear you described?

It is important to note that it is not only members of political opposition parties that are being suppressed. Human Rights Watch (HRW) has reported that soldiers will arbitrarily arrest and shoot "suspected thieves, smugglers, and other petty offenders, instead of prosecuting them." Most of the suspected thieves are first captured and arrested by civilian authorities and taken to military stations, where they are executed by soldiers. In many cases, individuals are captured in front of their family members, communities and friends. Audrey Wabwire spoke with Lewis Mudge, a Human Rights Watch researcher who stated, "People know this type of detention and torture happens in Rwanda, they are just too scared to talk about it openly. The best they can do is hope it doesn't happen to them."

However, given the deterioration in the rights of free press and a crackdown on journalists and human rights defenders cases of extrajudicial killings and arbitrary arrest are rarely reported on. Although the Rwandan constitution grants the media the "right to seek, receive, give and broadcast information and ideas", the genocide ideology law prohibits any promotion of ideas based on "ethnic, regional, racial, religious, language, or other divisive characteristics." This law is often cited when the government arrests, threatens, or silences dissenters. Therefore, crackdowns on civil society are often framed as combatting insurgency and divisive actions that threatens peace.

Repression in some countries has led to large-scale migration. How significant has migration from Rwanda been in the last decade or so, and what were the main reasons for the flight of citizens from the country?

Origin	Country/territory of asylum	Population start-2015 Total	of whom UNHCR-assisted	Group recognition	Temporary protection	Indiv. recognition	Voluntary repatriation Total	of whom UNHCR-assisted	Resettlement Total	of whom UNHCR-assisted	Cessation	Naturalization	Population end-2015 Total	of whom UNHCR-assisted
Russian Federation	Canada	1,315	-	-	-	54	-	-	-	-	-	117	1,175	-
Russian Federation	Denmark	1,261				54							1,028	
Russian Federation	France	13,544		-	-	1,084						154	14,195	
Russian Federation	Germany	4,598				988							3,858	
Russian Federation	Norway	2,328		-	-	13	-	-	-	-	-	-	1,851	-
Russian Federation	Poland	16,277				125					23		12,304	
Russian Federation	Sweden	2,014		-	-	142	-	-	-	-	-	-	2,003	-
Russian Federation	United States of America	8,163				335							5,805	
Rwanda	Canada	1,647		-	-	33	-	-	-	-	-	425	1,620	-
Rwanda	Congo, Republic of	9,104	9,104		12	18	38	112	114				8,549	8,549
Rwanda	Dem. Rep. of the Congo	38,978	7,008	-	-	6	5,024	5,024	9	9	-	-	245,052	137,000
Rwanda	France	2,833				62						95	2,795	
Rwanda	Malawi	1,980	1,980	-	-	90	-	-	30	30	-	-	2,116	2,116
Rwanda	South Africa	1,811	191			9							1,981	198
Rwanda	Uganda	14,312	14,312	-	-	166	-	-	9	9	-	-	14,714	14,714
Rwanda	United States of America	1,020				84							1,043	
Rwanda	Zambia	1,904	1,904	-	-	26	-	-	7	7	371	-	1,548	1,548

Unfortunately, adequate information about emigration from Rwanda is not available and this is not really an area of Amnesty International's competence.

Still, UNHCR has reported that during the start of 2015, there were a total of 72,642 Rwandan asylum seekers living in other countries. However, effective 30 June 2013 UNHCR asked countries to invoke a cessation of refugee status for those Rwandans who fled their homeland between 1959 and 1998, including the 1994 genocide, on the grounds that the conditions that drove them to seek protection abroad no longer exist. Many Rwandan refugees still fear persecution if they return home. Although, they can still seek an exemption or local integration, host countries are anxious to send the refugees back to Rwanda and are likely to avoid options that enable them to stay.

You accuse the previous Administration of being lax in its criticism of Rwandan human rights violations. What have you seen so far from the current Administration in this regard? Given its lack of ties to President Kagame, do you expect there will be a stronger line on such actions?

It is unlikely that President Trump will make US relations with Rwanda contingent on their human rights violations. Instead, it is likely that US policy with Rwanda will be based on the economic success of the country and how that success benefits US business or national security interests. President Trump's approach is to make sure that American interests come first. Hence, we assume that agreements and alliances will be entered into if they're in the interests of America's developmental and national security. This could be beneficial for Rwanda as both Presidents Trump and Kagame focus on promoting job creation and economic growth. Rwanda is a strong regional partner in Africa: they have one of the fastest growing economies In Africa and they contribute troops to UN peacekeeping and AU peace operations. Hence, it is possible that President Trump will focus more on the economic success that Rwanda has shown than the human rights violations the ruling party has committed.

www.ingramcontent.com/pod-product-compliance
Lightning Source LLC
Chambersburg PA
CBHW080858260726
48660CB00009B/3349